3op

PENGUIN BOOKS

WERE YOU STILL UP FOR PORTILLO?

Brian Cathcart was deputy editor of the *Independent on Sunday*. His book *Test of Greatness: Britain's Struggle for the Atom Bomb* was published in 1994, and he has recently finished writing an account of the murder of Stephen Lawrence and its consequences.

D1459304

Were You Still Up for Portillo?

BRIAN CATHCART

PENGUIN BOOKS

PENGUIN BOOKS

Published by the Penguin Group
Penguin Books Ltd, 27 Wrights Lane, London W8 5TZ, England
Penguin Books USA Inc., 375 Hudson Street, New York, New York 10014, USA
Penguin Books Australia Ltd, Ringwood, Victoria, Australia
Penguin Books Canada Ltd, 10 Alcorn Avenue, Toronto, Ontario, Canada M4V 3B2
Penguin Books (NZ) Ltd, 182–190 Wairau Road, Auckland 10, New Zealand

Penguin Books Ltd, Registered Offices: Harmondsworth, Middlesex, England

First published 1997
10 9 8 7 6 5 4

Set in 10.5/13.75pt Monotype Sabon
Typeset by Rowland Phototypesetting Ltd, Bury St Edmunds, Suffolk
Printed in England by Clays Ltd, St Ives plc

Contents

Illustrations

Acknowledgements

This book was not planned before the election; it could not have been. It had its origins in one of the millions of 'Wasn't it amazing?' conversations that took place in the weeks after 1 May, and I am grateful to Sue Matthias, who was the other half of that particular exchange. It is emphatically not a political reference book, but I owe a debt to several authors and editors in that field, notably Robert Waller and Byron Criddle, whose *Almanac of British Politics* is the *Gray's Anatomy* of its subject, and Colin Rallings and Michael Thrasher, editors of *The Media Guide to the New Parliamentary Constituencies*. Any mistakes, of course, are mine and not theirs. A number of others have helped in various ways, including Frances Benn, Charles Nevin, Barbara Gunnell, John Curtice, Leonard Doyle, Tracy Archbold, Robert and Judith Woodward, Paul Farrelly, Jan Dalley, Bill Crawford and the staff at the House of Commons Library, and I happily acknowledge the assistance of twenty or so of the winning candidates of the night, who may be identifiable from the text. My wife Ruth and sons Thomas and Patrick have endured a frenzy of obsessive activity with forbearance and good humour; to them I owe the most. And I must thank Nicole and Alex Segre, our hosts not only on this momentous election night but also on the rather different one in 1992. Finally, I pay tribute to the television teams; the coverage embraced the sublime and (at rare moments) the ridiculous, but it was public service broadcasting at its finest.

BRIAN CATHCART
August 1997

CHAPTER ONE

10 p.m. to 11 p.m.

*Exit polls – mood of denial – virtual Commons –
Paxman v. Portillo – race to be first – Mandelson's
pager – rogue Hezza – asteroid impact – long
memory – a result at last – Mullin's finest hour – the
number crunched – hemlock, Minister?*

It wasn't so much that they couldn't believe it; it was that they
couldn't grasp it, couldn't comprehend its meaning. At 10 p.m.
precisely on 1 May 1997, after a day of brilliant sunshine, the
polling stations closed and the ballot boxes were sealed. At the
same moment, and long before a single vote could have been
counted, the television channels brought astonishing news.

The BBC had questioned 14,000 people at 200 polling stations
and ITV had surveyed 15,000 in 100 constituencies. The two
exit polls were in broad agreement: Tony Blair's Labour Party
was heading for victory on a scale rarely seen before. A majority
of 159, said ITV. Nearly 200, said the BBC. Gosh. If ever a situation called for a Dimbleby this was it, and we had two of them.
But behind their respective veneers – David's seen-it-all-before
insouciance and Jonathan's well-scrubbed-schoolboy excitement
– even the Dimblebys were struggling with this one.

Both men, predictably, were aboard Captain Kirk's *Enterprise*.
David was on the bridge, at a large round desk with an 'E' on
it. Around him rose banks of flickering computer screens manned
by dozens of people in headphones, with a tellywall to bring in

the outside broadcasts and a lesser panel for graphics. Perched up at dress circle level like Lieutenant Uhura was Jeremy Paxman, in the little booth where he would hold his inquisitions. The colours were bright: oranges and purples with the blue-and-orange E logo sprinkled everywhere. It looked as though the BBC had blown a whole year's licence fee income from somewhere the size of, say, Bedford or Bolton. On ITV, brother Jonathan was to be found in a less familiar part of the spaceship: the cargo hold. A deep blue gloom surrounded him, and in the occasional pools of light could be seen silvery scaffolding. Behind that, apparently working in near-darkness, teams of number-crunchers were at their screens while, down at the far end, a few dozen members of the public were hidden, ready to air their views to Sue Lawley.

Upon these stages sat the two chips off the old Dimbleby block, smiling their different smiles and trying to come to terms with those exit poll figures. It was big. It was very big. Jonathan had a go. It was 'a massive majority', he said, 'a truly seismic shift in the politics of the nation'. David decided not to try anything flowery. It looked, he said, like 'a landslide', and he pointed out that the Conservative share of the vote was probably smaller than in any election since 1832. Then he left the grandiloquence to others.

We had been warned. In fact, if only we had believed all those other polls during the campaign we would not have been surprised by anything on election night. The exit poll findings were perfectly consistent with the campaign polls which, right to the end, showed Labour ahead by 12 per cent. Indeed, they were consistent with polls and local and European election results going back all the way to September 1992 and the ignominious exit of sterling from the European exchange rate mechanism on 'Black Wednesday'. That was the moment when, having seen John

Major and Norman Lamont admit that their economic policy was in ruins, the public turned against the Conservatives, and they never afterwards showed any serious sign of changing their minds. Through recession, negative equity, tax rises, sexual and financial scandals, BSE and endless Euro-rows, the British people maintained an air of downright disgust. Even economic recovery, with upward curves of growth and prosperity and downward curves of inflation and unemployment, stubbornly failed to alter their opinion. And yet almost nobody believed that, when it came to a general election, the voters would really let rip.

In part it was the experience of 1992. That election has been called the Waterloo of the polls – and with good reason, since the last campaign polls had been out by an astonishing 8 per cent and the exit polls had confidently predicted a hung parliament. In fact John Major emerged with an overall majority sufficient for a full five-year term. After a cock-up on that scale, no commentator with a head on his shoulders was going to give too much credence to a poll, particularly when its findings were so outlandish. But there was something else at work, both inside and outside the studios: denial. The degree to which the entire country refused to believe in the likelihood of change is something that will be difficult to communicate to anybody who did not live through the later Tory years. Whether you were Conservative, Labour or Liberal Democrat, the pattern of British politics had become so fixed that for most people a radical upset was simply beyond imagining.

This effect was most powerful for Labour supporters, still traumatized by 1992. They had seen power dashed from their grasp – against the odds and against the polls – by, of all people, John Major on his soapbox. Although the Labour Party's representation in parliament had jumped by 42 seats and the national vote by 1.5 million, it seemed the ultimate drubbing.

Something like grief and mourning followed, and the very mention of Basildon, the emblematic defeat of that night, was enough to stir these feelings again.

But it went still deeper. Labour, even in John Major's calamitous latter years, had got used to losing the argument. The parameters of political discussion remained those laid down by Margaret Thatcher – on Europe, on jobs, on tax, on unions – and it seemed impossible both to challenge the Tories and to win votes at the same time. Even when Conservatives were caught behaving badly, as in the Scott Report on arms sales to Iraq, no power could shift them. Ordinary Labour voters, despite themselves, were so used to the idea of defeat, of electoral disadvantage, of failure, that they could not bring themselves to believe it would stop. To imagine that it might end with the kind of result suggested by the exit polls seemed foolhardy, even irresponsible.

Liberal Democrats were, if anything, even more battered by history, having known false dawns in every decade since the war, and more heartbreaking near-misses at the polls than they could count. Yes, in the Major years they had made great inroads into Conservative territory in local elections and they had won some sensational by-election victories; but no, they could not easily bring themselves to believe this would really translate into more seats in parliament.

As for the Conservatives, everything you can say about the other two parties applies to them, only in reverse. So used were they to victory that they had little comprehension, let alone expectation, of defeat. After 18 years a minister was a Tory, a Tory was a minister; the reins of power seemed to be grafted to Conservative hands. As for the 1992 result, it did not seem so much a freak fourth term as proof that this was a party that had torn up the rule book and could stay for ever. This belief underlay

4

the party infighting over Europe; MPs and party members seemed to take re-election for granted.

So it was with long-handled tongs that the Dimblebys offered their exit polls to a doubting nation, repeating like a mantra the old politician's line that the only poll that counted was the election itself. The first result was still about an hour off, so they handed over to the wizards of graphics to show off their tricks.

When he is sitting behind a desk in the *Newsnight* studio, Peter Snow is an astute and determined journalist whose scrupulous attention to fact earned him the distinction of being denounced as a traitor by the *Sun* during the Falklands War. His silver hair, spectacles and worried expression give him gravitas, and his questioning has a seriousness and an intensity that are always impressive. When he is standing up, however, Snow can be a comedy turn. He has the body, walk and dress-style of Mr Bean and the sometimes manic enthusiasm for his subject of David Bellamy. The result is a jewel of television, and it is all the more precious because you feel you really shouldn't be enjoying anything so inappropriate. Bean-meets-Bellamy has performed three times in general elections to steadily increasing acclaim; but perhaps his finest hours on his feet were spent around the studio sandpit during the Gulf War, earnestly manoeuvring his Dinky tanks across desert wastes that measured all of eight feet across. Snow deserves better but, like it or not, he has become a light entertainment hero.

On this night to remember he was clad in a lightweight grey single-breasted suit which was over-generous in cut from shoulder to ankle, and the jacket pocket of which bulged in a manner likely to give Italian men nightmares. (What did he have in there, his car keys?) To the relief of some and the dismay of others, the

1. The BBC team: David Dimbleby (seated) ran the show with his
customary poise, just occasionally betraying a hint of surprise at what
was happening. Jeremy Paxman (right) played the observational
comedian, his well-rehearsed one-liners posing as questions. Peter Snow,
on graphics, confirmed his status as a British light entertainment hero.

brown brothel-creepers famously worn in 1987 made no return, and instead there were shiny black slip-ons. These now bore him smartly towards his big screen, where the pop-up politics commenced. 'This is just an exit poll but – my goodness! – it has to be terribly wrong for the Tories to win this election,' he said. '*Forty-seven per cent* the Labour share of the vote, if our exit poll is right. The best since 1966. *Twenty-nine per cent* the Conservatives . . . Eighteen per cent for the Liberal Democrats and 6 per cent for the others. Also that 18 per cent lead that Labour has over the Conservatives, *bigger even* than the record lead that Clement Attlee had in 1945. Now the changes that would represent over the last general election – Here they go! – Labour up 12 per cent and the Conservatives down 14 per cent . . .' With the words 'here they go' one coloured bar chart replaced another, and certainly it *was* clear: a white line, a large red block rising proud above it and an even larger blue block hanging forlornly beneath. 'Now let's bring down our swingometer and see what all that means. Here it comes!'

It came, but it was disappointing. Here was the quintessential instrument of election graphics and it had a flatness, a thinness which did scant justice to the subject. The swingometer goes all the way back to the 1950s, but it became a part of the national furniture in the hands of Bob Mackenzie in the 1960s. As recently as 1992 it was still operated manually, with a ten-foot arrow manipulated from above by unseen flunkeys. But now we were all-electronic, with little MPs in red and blue lined up on either side of the zero line in order of vulnerability. It was OK and, when it tipped to one side and displayed the numbers of casualties to relate to the swing, it was better; but somehow it didn't feel like a swingometer for the age of *Jurassic Park* and *Independence Day*.

'Just watch this,' said Snow, illuminating the implications of

7

the exit poll swing. The arrow swung towards the Tory side. 'On it goes. *On* and *on* and *on*. Look at those Conservative seats turning red, more than a hundred of them. Until you get to 13 per cent. Now that swing, if it was precisely accurate, uniform all over the country, would see Labour in with a majority of very nearly 200!' Then a note of caution: 'Don't forget these exit polls can be 2 per cent out – they can be even more than that if they're very wrong [conspiratorial chuckle] – but if they're 2 per cent out then the swing is 11 per cent. But look, Labour have a majority of more than 100 with an 11 per cent swing.' Now Snow began to hint at something even more amazing: if the poll was wrong it was because it was, if anything, *under*estimating the Tory disaster. 'We're getting messages from the detail of our exit poll that there's been some *tactical voting* going on, that the Liberal Democrats may do better than the national swing in the seats they're chasing and also that the Tories may be doing badly in their own seats. David.'

Over on ITV, Snow's rival of the night was Alastair Stewart, he of the exaggerated enunciation and strange teeth. 'His job is to bring clarity where otherwise confusion might reign,' Jonathan announced optimistically. As a TV turn Stewart on his own would be no match at all for the agile Snow; he's too neat and dapper, too controlled. But he had a secret weapon: his graphics were bigger, better, brasher. While Snow's were mainly two-dimensional and sensibly displayed on a wall behind him, Stewart, with all the casual panache of a stage magician, conjured up virtual reality. At a click of his fingers (and he really clicked them), he was able to summon up a virtual Commons chamber. One second there he was in the studio, perfectly normal, and the next he was walking down the aisle between those two familiar rows of green benches. Another click and Presto! the green benches were suddenly full of people, *moving* people – electronic

2. *The ITV team: Jonathan Dimbleby (left) played the anchor role, constantly reminding viewers that they were witnessing something extraordinary. Sue Lawley talked to a studio panel of voters. Michael Brunson, every politician's chum, kept up a stream of informed chat while Alastair Stewart found that even virtual reality graphics had to struggle to cope with the scale of change.*

MPs, he called them. It was breathtaking, like a trip into *Star Trek's* holodeck. Round one to Alastair.

What of the real-life politicians? Like everyone else, they were having trouble with those exit polls. Conservative chairman Brian Mawhinney smiled for all he was worth but made a poor fist of bravery. Speaking from his count in Cambridgeshire, he even seemed for an instant to admit defeat: 'The country has made its decision David. We have a new government.' Are you saying,

David asked in disbelief, that Labour has won? No, he was just trying to sound resonant. 'I'm saying that when the polls closed, all of those votes up and down the country constitute a new parliament, they constitute a new government. That may be a government led by John Major, or it may be a government led by Tony Blair. We will find the result fairly soon. I'm a patient man.'

John Prescott, Labour's Deputy Leader, popped up in Hull and seemed to accept victory. But the scale was beyond him and disbelief or exhaustion had chased away his usual bulldog smile. 'After losing four times,' he said, 'to win will be sufficient, make no mistake about that. We set our target for 90 seats; beyond that we'll have to wait and see. To win is important, and it looks as if we are going to win in very good fashion indeed.' He added boldly: 'This is a remarkable testament, I think, to the courage and vision of Tony Blair.'

Nothing much there. Surely this was a moment for Paxman to pull a rabbit from his hat and torture it? He had a go.

PAXMAN: Michael Portillo, are you going to miss the ministerial limo?

PORTILLO: As Brian Mawhinney said, I think we'll wait for the real results.

PAXMAN: If we believe these exit polls, you aren't in with a prayer. You're going down to the worst defeat in 150 years.

PORTILLO: I still think it's reasonable that we wait for the result tonight and not speculate about the theory. We're going to have a theory and we're going to have a fact tonight, so why don't we wait for the fact?

PAXMAN: What do you think was the biggest mistake in the campaign?

PORTILLO: Tony Blair telling fibs about pensions.

PAXMAN: In your own party?

PORTILLO: I think the thing the party needs to reflect on is that it's done itself no good by showing its divisions. That's what I think we need to reflect upon . . .

PAXMAN: You were saying that the big mistake of your party is that it appeared divided. If John Major is incapable of uniting the party, who would be?

PORTILLO: What I was saying before was that the party needs to be united and that's what the party needs to reflect upon. We don't know the result of the election yet, but whatever the result is, I'm sure the Conservatives would have done better than they will have done if, over the past few years, they had been more united.

PAXMAN: If you have gone down to this sort of defeat, can John Major stay as leader?

PORTILLO: We haven't got a result yet. John Major will consider the result when we have one.

PAXMAN: But on the basis of this prediction, it is likely that you will be one of the few Cabinet Ministers who keeps his seat. You, Michael Heseltine, John Major. But all those people like Michael Howard, Malcolm Rifkind, Michael Forsyth, they will all have gone.

PORTILLO: Well I'm not going to make any assumptions about the result, and I'm not quite clear why you're so impatient to do so.

PAXMAN: Michael Portillo, thank you. David?

David giggled mightily, but Portillo was not laughing. Far from enjoying all this clever badinage, the Secretary of State for Defence looked as though something he had eaten at dinner was disagreeing with him. His face was pasty, his expression was pained and his hands moved fretfully, at one moment performing an edgy drum-roll on his knees. No, this was not the Michael Portillo who had brought Conservative Party conferences to their feet with his cocky Labour-baiting and his insults to Brussels. Even Paxman's reassurance that his own seat was safe seemed to bring him little comfort.

Caution from politicians in such circumstances is wise and .

traditional, and Portillo had held the line, albeit at the cost of using some pretty unusual tenses ('the Conservatives would have done better than they will have done'). It was a surprise that it should have been the old warhorse Michael Heseltine, the Deputy Prime Minister, who went furthest. The man who two days earlier had predicted a Conservative majority of 60 seats told Radio 4: 'It doesn't look good. But then it did not look good at the last election at this stage . . . If the polls are right and we have actually lost then there have to be a lot of questions asked and a lot of answers produced.'

All this, of course, was merely treading water, filling time. When real results came in, the politicians could hardly refuse real comment – but when would they come? In one respect the delay was certain to be long, for the general election coincided with local government elections in many areas – for the most part, as it happened, Tory areas – and separating the ballot papers would slow things down. In another sense, however, the verdict of the voters was imminent, courtesy of the traditional Race To Be First, famously contested in the past by the likes of Billericay, Guildford and Torbay. This time the cast was different, since those seats all had local elections too. Hamilton South, the seat of George Robertson in Scotland, was having a go (the returning officer there was reported to be urging his staff to hurry up and 'beat the English'), and Wrexham was leading the charge for Wales. But it was the 1992 winner, Sunderland South, that was hot favourite, and with good reason.

If ever the words 'military precision' were appropriate, it was in describing Sunderland's approach to the count. At the stroke of 10 p.m., 65 vans had leapt into action, whisking the 70 ballot boxes from the polling stations through the town to the Crowtree Leisure Centre. Police were on hand to usher them into bus-only lanes for added speed, and they overrode the traffic lights outside the Centre to prevent logjams. At the loading bay, 40 runners in red sweatshirts grabbed the boxes and rushed them in – these boxes were, by choice, old-style metal ones rather than the modern plastic, because experiments had shown that access to the seal was easier. As soon as the seals were cut the contents were 'cascaded' on to tables for the 140 counters. So smoothly did it all run that this first phase was over, and all 70 boxes had been emptied, in just 10 minutes 30 seconds.

The counters were mostly bank clerks in real life, and they operated in self-selected teams of four because, as a Sunderland official put it, 'people work better with their chums'. Some time in advance, a bright spark among them had observed that, compared with banknotes, the ballot papers were like cardboard to count, so some further experiments were conducted and they switched to a lighter paper. Perhaps Sunderland's most ambitious step was to include the voters in the effort. Many of us, for reasons of secrecy or psychological disturbance, like to fold our ballot papers more than once – some people get them down to the size of postage stamps. Not in Sunderland. At every polling station there, the presiding officer asked electors to fold only once, north to south, to assist with a speedy count (there is no record of what happened to those who failed to co-operate, but they probably didn't have their bins emptied for a month). The final touch was the spoiled ballot papers: these are normally stacked up during counting, and at the end the returning officer goes through them with the candidates' agents to ensure everybody agrees they are not valid. Sunderland would not wait. Throughout the count the agents were on hand to discuss each spoiled vote as it came in, so that no time would be wasted in haggling at the end.

It was all as slick as a Tony Blair press conference, with nothing left to chance. Why, you may ask, do they bother? The red sweatshirts provide a clue. This is a modern-day *Jeux Sans Frontières*, a once-in-five-years *It's An Election Knockout*. For the hell of it, and a dash of civic pride, half a dozen towns around Britain hold a silly race and, having succeeded once, it seems, no one drops out of the game. In 1997 Sunderland didn't just want to be first, though; they wanted to break the record set by Billericay in 1959, of 57 minutes from gun to tape. And they were well on their way.

All this the cameras observed in wonderment and, when they were not watching Sunderland perform, they would pass the time by hopping around the country to show off how many outside broadcast sites were on tap – 'literally hundreds', said David Dimbleby, before confessing that that was an exaggeration. One such tour gave us a nice perspective on New Labour. In Birmingham the camera followed Clare Short, in bright-red trouser-suit, strolling around the counting centre on the arm of a man young enough to be her son. On closer scrutiny he proved indeed to be her son: Toby, the boy she had given up for adoption at birth and whom she had rediscovered a few months before the election – just in time to convert him from Tory to Labour (he had grown up an accountant).

From Birmingham we hopped across to Stevenage, where a well-groomed couple sat in silence before the camera, studiously not looking into it. This was Barbara Follett, the Labour candidate and former image-maker to the front bench, with her fourth husband, the thriller-writer and New Labour enthusiast, Ken. Ms Follett, like Ms Short, was in red, in her case a red that gave the television screen the shivers. From the woman who put the Labour front bench into their dark suits this was a lapse, but a rare one. As we watched, she turned to her husband and her lips formed the words: 'A kiss?' Ken obliged with a firm peck. 'Oh my goodness me,' said David Dimbleby, back in the studio, 'did they know we were watching?'

Next came Hartlepool, and another juicy moment in the interplay of screen with life. Here we watched Labour's campaign director joking with onlookers at his own count. Dimbleby observed: 'Peter Mandelson, who apparently escaped a terrible car accident yesterday. He's the man who really constructed the whole of this campaign. He was responsible for every twist and turn of manipulation. He's known as the Prince of Darkness.' As we heard these words, we saw Mandelson reach into a pocket, pull out a pager and look down to read from the little screen. Dimbleby was watching. 'And there he is, looking at the pager with messages coming through – probably saying, "You're on BBC1. Smile." They control things so closely.' Mandelson did not smile. But as if to prove how closely things were controlled, when the camera switched to Brent East, the last stop of this little tour, somehow it just couldn't find the face of the Labour MP there. That MP is Ken Livingstone, popular left-winger and no friend of Mandelson's.

With Sunderland now just a few minutes from declaring, David Dimbleby turned for a final few words to Anthony King, who long ago had replaced the great Bob Mackenzie as the tame Canadian professor in the BBC team. A sensational night, Tony? 'Absolutely. Landslide is much too weak a word for it. I offer you the following metaphor: it's an asteroid hitting the planet and destroying practically all life on Earth.' Since none of us could remember what that was like, he groped back into the more immediate past for something we could compare it with. First: 'There's really been nothing like it since the Second World War.' Then: 'Nothing like it in this century.' And finally, he screwed up his face: 'The Conservatives are doing horrendously badly; as you said a few moments ago, it looks like

3. Peter Mandelson, Labour's campaign director.

being their worst night possibly since the Great Reform Act of 1832.'

When it came to history, ITV had it in the flesh. David Butler, the veteran analyst who was once Richard Dimbleby's foil ('Butler!' he used to cry when he wanted numbers crunched), was on hand to recall that the forecast swing of 12 per cent would match 1945, 'the first election I saw as an adult'. He went on: 'But of course it's nothing to 1931, when I remember going with my mother to vote at the age of seven, and in fact there were 500 seats for the Conservatives.' Alas, he had no memories to offer us of that corking election back in 1832, but he conceded to Jonathan Dimbleby that even for an old-timer this looked like being 'a turnover of monumental scale'.

Seconds out from the first result, Anthony King told us what to look out for: 'If Chris Mullin has got round about 34,000 votes then that means that Labour is in for a huge win tonight and that our exit poll is broadly right. Listen to the returning officer, wait for the Chris Mullin figure – he's the sitting Labour Member of Parliament. His vote last time was under 30,000; it may go up to a very much higher figure, and if it does then it does look as though Labour is going to make it.'

In Sunderland we saw the candidates in their bright rosettes huddle with the returning officer, then break and file up on to the platform, where the returning officer made his way to the podium. Then this: 'Ladies and gentlemen, if I can have your attention, I shall now read the results for the election in the Sunderland South constituency. I hereby give notice that the total number of votes for each candidate at the election was as follows: John Anthony Lennox, Liberal Democrat, four thousand, six hundred and six; Christopher John Mullin, the Labour Party candidate, twenty-seven thousand, one hundred and seventy-four [loud cheer from the floor]; Timothy John Schofield, Conservative Party candidate, seven thousand five hundred and thirty-six [more cheers]; Margaret Anne McQuillan Wilkinson, UK Independence Party, six hundred and nine. And that Christopher John Mullin has been duly elected to serve as the member for the Sunderland South constituency [loud cheers again].' There had been a swing to Labour from the Conservatives of 10.5 per cent, and Mullin's majority had leapt from 14,000 to 20,000.

Less than half an hour earlier, Chris Mullin had been expecting something rather different. He knew, of course, that *he* would win, for Sunderland South is rock-solid Labour country. What he didn't know was that his result would offer a first glimpse of something sensational. 'I thought we would win by twenty to thirty seats, that was all,' he said later. 'Nothing prepared me for what happened. During the campaign I saw no particular enthusiasm among my own electorate. In Sunderland, of course, the question is not so much who to vote for as whether to vote at all, and my canvassing had been directed mainly towards those people who tend not to. It was actually quite worrying. I've been involved in every election since 1970 and I've never seen such apathy and indifference.'

Armed with this experience, Mullin had resisted any temptation to believe the exit polls, but as he watched the rapid counting in Sunderland it dawned on him that things were not as he expected. 'The moment I knew we had a landslide was at about 10.20 p.m., when I looked at the table and saw the Conservative still on 6,000 votes while I was heading for 26,000. Then I knew the Tory vote had simply collapsed.' When the returning officer called the candidates together to give them the final figures he was still astonished, although his expression clearly showed his delight.

Chris Mullin is a backroom politician, to some the epitome of the old, serious, Bennite Left from which he sprang. By the standards of the back benches he has a lot to brag about: as journalist and MP he did more than almost anyone else to secure the release of the Birmingham Six, and he was the author of a genuine best-seller and hit television drama, *A Very British Coup*. But he is no strutting Jeffrey Archer, and though he has drifted from his earlier hard-left attitudes (he backed Tony Blair for the leadership) he remains a sober, independent voice on the Labour back benches.

Wearing the broadest of smiles, this low-key character now stepped forward to face the biggest audience of his life. From his jacket pocket he pulled out the speech he had prepared. It had been written with less dramatic circumstances in mind – that 30-seat victory he had expected – and it was all the better for that. 'Ladies and gentlemen, friends,' he said, in a voice as clear as a bell, 'it is absolutely clear from this result that in a few hours from now 18 years of Conservative rule are going to come to an end [cheers], and I am proud that the people of Sunderland, who during those 18 years suffered more than most, are leading the way. Tonight marks the beginning of a new era, a return to

4. *Chris Mullin, victorious in Sunderland South.*

one-nation politics. From now on Britain will be governed in the interests of all its citizens, and not just in the interests of the fortunate [sustained applause].'

Abraham Lincoln could hardly have done it better. Gracious in tone, that short speech neatly turned the page from the old to the new, acknowledging at once past hardship and present joy. It had a nod to his constituents and a nod ('one-nation politics') to New Labour. It was also elegant. As he reached the end of the last sentence most of his listeners must have expected him to say '. . . and not just the interests of the *rich*', or even '. . . and not just the interests of *a bunch of selfish fat cats*'. But he didn't; the word he used was dignified rather than defiant, and it had been selected with care. Mullin had remembered a remark by Michael Frayn in 1974, when he said he was going to vote Labour 'to protect the unfortunate from the tyranny of the fortunate'. Now in 1997, 'fortunate' seemed right.

Viewers of the BBC at this stage might have been forgiven some confusion about the scale of the victory; after all, Professor King had told them that Mullin would need 34,000 votes if Labour were really on course for a landslide, yet here he was, jubilant with only 27,000. The explanation, as David Dimbleby was quick to point out, was a slump in turnout. Everybody was down: Labour by 2,000, the Conservatives by 7,000 and the LibDems by 1,000 votes. In fact turnout in Sunderland South had fallen to a historic low of 59 per cent. Was the deciding factor a decision by Tory voters simply to stay at home in even greater numbers than the others, or was something more complex going on?

In the ITV studio political editor Michael Brunson, whose lop-sided smile and shock of black hair recall Leslie Crowther in his *The Price is Right* years, opted for the complex. It was, he said, 'the Tories' worst nightmare': a straight switch from

Conservative to Labour. And psephologist David Cowling agreed: 'It was a feature of the last election in hundreds and hundreds of seats that the Labour vote went up, the Liberal Democrats down and the Conservatives stayed solid. Here [in Sunderland] we have seen what appears to have been a direct transfer from Conservative to Labour.' And the bar charts seemed to confirm it: in terms of the proportion of votes cast, Labour was 10 per cent up in Sunderland South, and the Conservatives were 10 per cent down.

Barely noticed was the triumph of Sunderland's counters. Not only were they first, but they had shattered the record of 57 minutes, producing their declaration (judged from the moment the returning officer started to speak) in 46 minutes flat. Eddie Waring would have had the words for it.

Peter Snow, at the swingometer, fed in 'the first real result to grind our teeth into', and at first the picture was anticlimactic: a Labour majority, not of nearly 200, but of just over 100. But Snow reminded us that the exit poll suggested the swing would be greater in seats the Tories were defending, which would mean a substantially greater number of Conservative losses.

And David Dimbleby seemed to believe him, finally producing some hyperbole to match the occasion. 'We're on track,' he said, 'for a Labour landslide on a gargantuan scale.'

Robin Oakley, the BBC political editor, joined in, observing that for the Tories 'it's not so much a case of back to the drawing board as buy a new drawing board . . . It means that Mr Major will depart, and probably fairly quickly.'

Up in the dress circle Paxman cocked an eyebrow. 'Michael Portillo,' he asked, 'are you ready to drink hemlock yet?'

CHAPTER TWO

11 p.m. to Midnight

Tebbit's poison – the art of Edwina – some Dunkirk
spirit – a dicey dozen – Hamilton – 'Mr Buchan'
– comic relief – waiting, waiting – a smile from Gordon
Brown – Wrexham – casting off the coat of caution –
curtains in Sedgefield – deep in fertilizer.

Others at this time had poison in mind, but they were not planning to use it on themselves. Lord Tebbit, with characteristic charm, observed that during the election he had no idea who was running the Conservative campaign and he didn't think Brian Mawhinney did either. And Nicholas Winterton, the Tory MP for Maccles-field, blamed it all on Ken Clarke who, he said, would be 'reviled in history for his actions'.

Michael Brunson, somehow taking soundings among Conservatives between his frequent appearances on screen, reported that the hunt for scapegoats had indeed begun, but that it was not Clarke and Mawhinney who were in danger, it was Euro-sceptics like Tebbit and Winterton. Brunson (the man to whom, incidentally, John Major made his famous remark about 'bas-tards' in his Cabinet) predicted that there would be 'intense anger' against 'those who caused all the splits'. At which point who should pop up but Edwina Currie, scourge of the sceptics and incorrigible rubber of salt into party wounds?

Edwina was waiting patiently in Derbyshire South for a per-sonal defeat she had long expected – as early as 1994 she was so

5. Edwina fills the screen from Derbyshire South.

certain of it that she stood for the European Parliament in the vain hope of finding another berth. Now, as she whiled away the time at her final count, she strove to live up to those two labels she had earned in her 14 years of national politics: 'colourful' and 'controversial'. For colour, she was a sight to fill the screen, indeed the whole living-room. Her jacket was bright pink, and struggling with it were two strings of pearls, a pair of large, pearl-and-gold earrings, a gold brooch of the Palace of Westminster portcullis, a blue rosette and a pink flower arrangement at the throat that was so enormous only Edwina's face could have upstaged it. The lips and eyebrows, as ever, owed more to art than to nature.

As for the controversial stuff, she finds it so easy. What had gone wrong, she was asked, policy or presentation? 'I think it's been a problem with everything. One thing is for certain. I've

23

always said that the electorate here has never voted into office a party that is antagonistic to Europe. That looks as if it's happening again, that moving Euro-sceptic has done us no good whatsoever, and the electorate have rejected us.' And what about the future of the Prime Minister? 'It will be a tragedy for the man,' she replied movingly, and then: 'My preference is that we should get the leadership contest under way as soon as this election is out of the way.' Her favourite? 'Somebody who is wisely and sensibly pro-European and can carry the nation forward' – Ken Clarke. As for the rest, she offered three acid thoughts: it could be Michael Heseltine, 'if there are no worries about his health', or Gillian Shephard, 'if she holds her seat', and finally this. 'What I'm absolutely certain about is that an anti-European, very right-wing, rather extreme personality will simply make sure that we go into the next election campaign in exactly the same sort of state we've gone into this one.'

Down in London, Michael Dobbs, the Conservative Party Deputy Chairman and author of the political thriller *House of Cards*, was thinking acid thoughts about Currie. 'Perhaps I can thank Edwina for all the helpful advice she has given to us during the campaign,' he said, 'and then perhaps get on to some more serious subjects.' Dobbs is basically a spin doctor, someone whose job is to find words that accentuate the positive and explain away (or blame somebody else for) the negative. On this occasion he clearly had a job on his hands, for his tone and demeanour left no doubt that he saw defeat as inevitable even if he didn't know its scale. The course he chose showed his perception-management skills at their best. It might be called the Dunkirk spirit ploy. He stood before us a proud man, he announced. 'When we fought the 1979 election we took over a country which was crucified by discontent, split apart, and if we are handing the country over to another government tonight, it's a country which has a strong economy and there are not riots in the streets.' In other words, we may have been defeated tonight, but in an odd way it is a victory . . .

To the obvious question – if you were doing so brilliantly, why are the voters throwing you out? – Dobbs produced another fine riposte: 'I suspect there is simply a mood in the country for change. There are no great demands for a Labour government out there. There are no riots against the Conservative government. There is simply a decision that it is time for a change, and that is I think proving to be a pretty overwhelming appeal.' Far from screwing up, he was saying, the Conservatives had done everything right, and it was for their very success that they were being punished.

The Deputy Prime Minister and First Secretary of State now swept into Central Office past the billboard announcing 'Britain is booming. Don't let Labour blow it' and soon afterwards on to the television screens of the nation. Michael Heseltine (for it was he) was asked about that 60-seat win he had been predicting. 'I fight to win,' came the reply. 'Any hesitancy or doubt gives quite the wrong signal to your many millions of supporters.' You half expected him to wink. Then he slipped into Dobbs mode – proud, defiant and almost ecstatic in his praise for John Major: 'Historians are going to give him the highest plaudits for the transformation he has brought about and the rocks that he has planted upon which we can make progress . . . Nobody, nobody can deny the quality of the economic infrastructure that he has put in place.'

While senior Tories were writing their government's obituary in the most glowing terms they could find, excited telly people were busy working out just how many senior Tories were for the chop. Peter Snow showed off his 'Dicey Dozen' Conservatives – not, he stressed, that he was suggesting *for a moment* that their conduct was in any way dicey, just their predicament. In what was probably the most unsuccessful graphic of the whole night, 12 cut-out people stood in a queue leading up to a white cliff. The idea was that landslides of various sizes, illustrated by the cliff falling over, would bury different numbers of these dicey people, starting with the nearest. The trouble was that Peter's cliff wasn't nearly big enough, so that while you could just about imagine it falling on Scottish Secretary, Michael Forsyth, who was at the head of the queue, it would have had to get up and walk in order to reach, say, Sebastian Coe, who was sixth in line. Still, the point was made: not only were well-known backbenchers such as Edwina Currie, Tony Marlow and Nicholas Budgen under threat, so too were big hitters like Forsyth, Ian Lang and Malcolm Rifkind. In the event of a really big swing, David Mellor and William Waldegrave were in danger. And Michael Howard, the Home Secretary, could even be at risk from the LibDems. As time passed and tip-offs came in from the constituencies, more big names joined the list of Diceys, including John Gummer, Tony Newton and Roger Freeman. Most unbelievable of all was the possibility raised by Brunson on ITV that Finchley, the former seat of Margaret Thatcher which he described as 'the temple of Conservatism', might tumble.

This was all very well, but you didn't have to have a long political memory to know that it was one thing to project a statistical swing across the country but quite another to put scalps in the bag. Occasionally, yes, as with Shirley Williams in 1979 or Chris Patten in 1992, a minister had fallen in a general election, but it was a real rarity. Big names had a habit of hanging on, saved by their high profiles, by their personal followings, or by luck. Labour and LibDem supporters also remembered the 'bottling-out' factor which had made electors change their minds in the polling booths last time and vote at the last moment for the devil they knew. If they did that again this time, surely it was more likely to happen in the marginals, where votes made a difference, than in safe seats such as Sunderland? If what you wanted was to see the Conservatives defeated, the Dicey Dozen looked like 12 hostages to fortune.

And there were some straws in the wind that looked comforting for Conservatives. Out in the country, reporters kept finding Tory Party officials at the counts who were less gloomy than Dobbs or Heseltine. In Huntingdon, an unnamed adviser to the Prime Minister was reported as saying that she thought a hung parliament might be on the cards, but she could not accept the idea of a landslide. In Mitcham and Morden, where the former minister Dame Angela Rumbold was defending a slim majority, another Tory source insisted his information showed that not only would she get back, she could even increase her majority. There was similar talk in East Anglia. It might be bad over in *that* constituency, the officials would say, but our figures here show something *much* more promising. Even Malcolm Rifkind, number eight on Snow's list, turned up with his Jiminy Cricket smile and talked of 'some positive signs'.

Rifkind's grin was the cause of some comment. David Dimbleby thought it surprising that the Foreign Secretary should look happy in such circumstances, 'but then he's a stoic politician and a Scottish lawyer to boot, so probably he can put on a good face'. Brother Jonathan raised the matter with the man himself, and was told: 'I always have a broad smile on my face when I'm about to be interviewed by you. It cheers me up no end.' Ask a silly question . . . Rifkind went on: 'I have represented a marginal constituency all my political career and each time I've been told I'm about to lose it and each time I haven't, so I'm full of incurable optimism.'

*

By now we had another result. Scotland's *It's A Knockout* entry, Hamilton South, declared 20 minutes after Sunderland and brought us another smile, this time remarkable for appearing on the smallest mouth in British politics, that of Labour's Scottish spokesman, George Robertson. Robertson, 49, a policeman's son, had carried Labour's flag in Scotland since 1993, and it had been no easy task. The party is so dominant north of the border and has been for so long that it is effectively the establishment there, and it always ran the risk that a vote for change in Scotland could be a vote for somebody else. At the same time, focusing anger on the government in London was always perilously similar to mobilizing anti-English sentiment, particularly since the Conservatives were down to just a handful of seats in Scotland. These factors complicated the devolution debate mightily, and Labour had more than once got itself into a muddle. In the end, it fudged the issue by promising a referendum after the election, a piece of procrastination which had the virtue of shielding the party from the pro-union challenge of the Conservatives, but the vice of exposing it to the more frontal (and possibly more honest) attack of the Scottish National Party. It was a fine gamble and Robertson was known to be uncomfortable with it; would it pay off?

Hamilton South, as safe a Labour seat as they come, was never going to provide a complete answer, but it gave Labour every ground for confidence. Robertson's notional 1992 majority after allowing for boundary changes had been 13,000; by the time the returning officer had finished speaking it was almost 16,000. Better still, both the Conservatives and the SNP were down by a third. Robertson stepped to the microphone and spoke off the cuff: 'This evening we're here at a historic time, when a historic decision has been taken for our whole country. It is clear from these first two results and indeed from the exit polls that there is going to be a Labour government in this country after 18 years and that this country will move in a completely new and better direction. In this campaign in Scotland the Scottish Labour Party did it *with* Scotland, and we did it *for* Scotland. And for all the people of Scotland as well. And as we move forward now into a completely new era for our country, the people have placed their trust in us.'

ITV sought an SNP reaction from Alex Salmond, whom a stumbling Jonathan Dimbleby introduced as 'Mr Buchan up in Banff and Buchan'. The SNP leader laughed unconvincingly and began: 'Jonathan – or maybe I should call you David?' He went on to state, quite accurately, that Hamilton South was not an SNP target and that nothing much could be read into it. Everything, he insisted, pointed to his party gaining seats, and he observed that the constituency of Glasgow Govan was 'on a knife edge this evening'. It was typical Salmond, brisk and abrasive, and it ended with a sheepish Jonathan promising to remember the man's name in future. This brought the chilling reply: 'And I will remember yours.'

A word now about Frank Skinner. The comedian and football enthusiast had been recruited by the BBC for the night to act as comic relief, popping up every now and then to punctuate all those grim interviews and statistics. If ever proof was needed that the great BBC News and Current Affairs empire lacked an understanding of humour, this was it. The station that brought you Peter Snow, last seen in Biggles mode introducing his 'Labour targets fly-around', and Jeremy Paxman, perhaps the country's leading observational comedian, had no need for a humour ghetto. Moreover Skinner was an odd choice, since his chat-show interview with Tony Blair some months earlier had been a cringing milestone in blandness. In the event he was not let loose on real politicians, but he was still hopelessly out of place, not least because his contributions were treated with such disdain by David Dimbleby that you thought there must be bad blood between them.

We first met the comic choppering northwards over Pontefract ('Must pop down for some cakes!'), when he informed us he was our bit of rough for the night and would be introducing us to some Yorkshire 'characters'. Handing back, he observed that it was still light where he was and wasn't that weird? It was a harmless enough remark, requiring Dimbleby to make some simple response such as 'Weird indeed'. Even a smile might have sufficed. But no. He could not have been more deadpan if he had been welcoming us back from a news update on bloodshed in Zaire.

Next, Skinner was in a pub somewhere interviewing two lookalikes, one Major, one Blair, about their respective prospects, and then for some reason asking them to dance together. Again Dimbleby played the spoilsport. And it got worse. Skinner's third contribution came from a back room in Harrogate Town Hall, where he had bearded the mayor ('Nice necklace!'). They managed a jolly enough bit of banter about how the declaration could be livened up with funny pronunciations of Norman Lamont's name, and then Skinner concluded with the remark: 'You knew where you were with Mrs Thatcher. It was just being there without a paddle that I didn't like.' It was a good joke to hand back on. How did David Dimbleby respond? A funereal face and: 'Ken Skinner, there.' You had the feeling his heart wasn't in it.

All this – Skinner, Currie, Salmond – was still verbal thumb-twiddling, distractions contrived to fill the time. Where were the results? That business of separating county council from general election votes was proving very laborious. By 11.30 p.m. we still had only a measly two, both safe Labour seats and both pretty limited in the amount that could be read into them. Neither Sunderland nor Hamilton was anywhere near 'The Battleground', the swing seats which would decide the result, and until we had heard from these we were little better off than we had been at 10 p.m. For in those constituencies − mostly outer-city areas and the larger towns − the election had been very different from elsewhere. Labour, as John Prescott pointed out, had identified 90 'key seats' into which it had poured all its efforts for nearly two years. Everything outside was either assumed to be safe or was written off as un-winnable, and party workers, wherever they came from, were pushed into the key seat drive. From one year before the election, in Operation Victory, Labour attempted the huge feat of interviewing 80 per cent of key seat voters by telephone or face to face, to identify party supporters who could be mobilized and to swing voters who could be persuaded. And once John Major had called the election these people were relentlessly leafleted and telephoned in the drive to GOTV − get out the vote.

While Labour attacked, the Conservatives threw up sandbags around these seats, ready to fight on Labour's chosen ground. The effect, seen before in 1992 when the Tories defended success-fully, was to concentrate the election, so that the real struggle was not countrywide but took place in a few areas where a small number of swing voters mattered. By some counts, as few as 60,000 votes would determine who would govern the nearly 60,000,000 people of the United Kingdom. Now, on election night, we needed to hear what *they* had decided, not the people in safe seats whose votes were taken for granted. But as the thriller-writers know, the longer the delay the greater the suspense; waiting for a marginal result was turning into a particularly cruel form of torture.

If supporters of the opposition parties were biting their nails and if Tories of all ranks were caught between hope, anger and despair, there was one group of people who were really enjoying themselves, and that was the Labour leadership. Landslide or no, they were in and they seemed to know it. What is more, they could no longer help showing it. Nowhere was this transformation more evident than on the visage of the sitting Labour MP for Dunfermline East, Gordon Brown. Brown by name and brown by nature, this mournful undertaker of a man had spent years trying to elevate grimness to a political virtue. Now he appeared before us metamorphosed into a jubilant schoolboy, with two rows of gleaming white teeth bisecting his face. He was barely recognizable.

How reassuring it was to discover that his speaking manner had not changed correspondingly. Brown is the most on-message of all Labour's on-message spokesmen, the most disciplined and in consequence often the least exciting performer. His technique is to hook tried-and-tested party slogans together one after another until he has created something resembling a verbal freight train. One such train now rolled by, as he told a Dimbleby: 'It's not just a rejection of the Conservative Party / it's a vote for New Labour / for a new type of politics / for equipping this country properly for the future / and for tackling the very real social problems. / We stood on a manifesto for change and we will honour that. / We will build a new trust with the British people . . . / I think people have been captured by the message that Tony Blair put across / that we can transform the politics of this country / we can break away from the old divisions.' And so on.

Instinctively or by co-ordination, senior Labour figures were all trotting out the line that, however it might look, the voters were not simply punishing the Tories but were enchanted with New Labour. On ITV Julia Somerville quoted the spin doctor David Hill as saying: 'The whole thing is about Tony Blair: Tony Blair's leadership, Tony Blair's magnificent campaign, Tony Blair's ability to persuade the electorate that Labour really has changed.' Peter Mandelson beamed down from Hartlepool the message: 'What swung it was New Labour. People have been coming towards us steadily over the past ten years, but it was the transformation of the Labour Party, the rebirth of the Labour Party in the last two or three years, that really clinched it.' The true message here was this: these men wanted us to think that it was their cleverness and their determination to change their party that had 'swung it', not Conservative sleaze or incompetence, and not some ephemeral public feeling that it was time for a change. They were claiming ownership of the victory.

Another result came in, this time from the Welsh entry in the race, Wrexham, another safe Labour seat. For all their haste to finish, however, the Wrexham team seemed to get bogged down just a yard short of the tape. The returning officer marched the six candidates up on to the platform in front of a large sign saying 'Wrexham / Wrecsam', and the watching television producers, not unreasonably, took it as a signal to go live for the declaration. But the result wasn't ready and we had that broadcaster's nightmare: a void to fill. David Dimbleby pattered on: 'This is north-east Wales and it's a safe Labour seat. It's a mining area and it's held by Dr John Marek, who's actually a mathematician, rather a quiet presence in the House of Commons. For 17 years or so he taught mathematics down at the university in Aberystwyth.' Jonathan, perhaps aware that MPs do not come much duller than Marek, tried a different tack, but the effect was of desperation: 'Anyway, this town is the largest town in

Wales. It used to be a coalmining town. It has the oldest football club in Wales, as well. And it is the home of the International Eisteddfod, and last year Pavarotti no less attended the fiftieth anniversary of the Eisteddfod. It was a huge occasion.'

After three false starts we got what we had come for. Labour won easily, there was a slump in the Conservative vote and another low turnout. The swing, however, was a less-than-gargantuan 7 per cent, way below the 10–12 per cent Anthony King had told us to watch out for. In Welsh terms this would be enough to remove seven of the eight Tory MPs in the principality, but over the rest of Britain, as the swingometers quickly showed, it would give Labour a majority of fewer than 70. Oops. With Sunderland North landing moments later (the same counting team in Sunderland was both first and fourth nationally), there was now an average swing over the first four seats of 9 per cent, or a majority of under 100. On this basis it looked more like a dicey half-dozen than a dozen.

In the studios, however, they seemed to know better. Nothing, and certainly not a few real results, was going to shake them off their beloved exit polls at this stage. Professor King went so far as to say that the results confirmed everything he expected, while Robin Oakley had a brisk answer for those reporters in the field who suggested that the Tories might do better than the polls suggested: 'I think that's what they're being told by Tory Party workers and Tory Party agents.' The Tories themselves might be dupes, he speculated, because the quality of canvasser had gone down the drain since the old days, and of course the voters on their doorsteps couldn't be trusted at all. 'The British are a very polite nation,' Oakley observed. 'They don't like to say they're not going to vote for somebody. And when you speak to them afterwards they say, "I wouldn't vote for that shower if they came down the driveway with a barrow full of fivers".'

Another place where, by midnight, the doubters held no sway was Sedgefield in County Durham, the constituency of Tony Blair. Here, at the Trimdon Labour Club, tickets had been oversubscribed ten times and the party faithful had their eyes down for a serious night of celebration. From the local leisure centre, where the count was under way, ITV's Mark Webster reported eloquently on a change of mood: 'Labour activists on the floor are starting to believe what they didn't dare believe before, that victory is really going to be theirs. They are casting off the coat of caution they have been wearing for the past month and they're starting to say, "My goodness, this really is looking like our night".'

The BBC, meanwhile, was trying to peek through a window into the former colliery manager's house which is the Blairs' Sedgefield home, but, just as we cut to the scene, a suited arm inside the house reached across and pulled the curtains closed. Spoilsport. We hopped to weightier matters elsewhere, but five minutes later we were back, because somebody had opened the curtains. (Now why would they do that?) Beyond a vase of flowers we glimpsed the back of a man in a suit. 'There he is!' David Dimbleby said triumphantly, 'the man who will be Prime Minister tomorrow.' But, as we watched, another man came into view, and this second man was clearly Tony Blair. So who was that first man who was to be PM within hours? None other than Alastair Campbell, the Labour leader's media minder and a former *Daily Mirror* journalist. Was it he who had closed the curtains and then opened them again? If it was, he performed a public service, for we were privileged to watch as both men engaged in a lengthy primp before a mirror in the hall. In the studio David Dimbleby was smiling. 'Just a brief glimpse of Tony Blair,' he said.

A few minutes later, the Labour leader was through the front door and walking briskly past the policemen with machine-guns to greet a well-behaved group of 20 or so admirers, about half of them children, many in baseball caps. Shaking hands with both hands, one over the other, he worked his way along and then, as a small cheer went up, he waved, turned on his heel and made for his red Jaguar. Someone asked a question and he replied: 'Let's just wait and see, shall we?' He leapt in beside his older son, Euan, and his wife, Cherie, and was off to the count.

Down in London at about that moment, Richard Branson was arriving at the Royal Festival Hall, where a Labour celebration was just beginning. And in the BBC studio Jeremy was up to his tricks again: 'Well now, Cecil Parkinson, you're chairman of a fertilizer firm. How deep is the mess you're in at present?'

CHAPTER THREE

Midnight to 1 a.m.

Desperate moments – magnanimous Cook – Edgbaston
at last – a 'leper' bows out – pizza party –
LibDem gain – exorcism in Basildon – Budgen
beaten – swingometer trouble – Branson's vote –
sweeping up the leafies.

As the clock ticked past midnight and Friday, 2 May, began, things were getting desperate in the studios. Every single analyst had said his piece; every reporter in the field with anything remotely interesting to report had done it; all the graphics had been put through their paces and every formula of speculative hyperbole had been tested. We were subjected to a pitiful spectacle: before our very eyes, people whose entire lives revolved around talking politics were running out of meaningful things to say. Jonathan in particular was flailing, like one of those feeble guest panellists on *Just a Minute*. Having filled us in about Pavarotti in Wrexham, he was now rabbiting on about Clare Short, proclaiming earnestly that she was 'one of the politicians whom men and women up and down the country love because they think she speaks her mind, and yet in politics that's not always an advantage'. Deviation!

It wasn't much better on the other side; they didn't have any more informative results either. Soon both channels, were lovingly following every step of Tony Blair's entry into the Sedgefield count. No angle could be missed. Each had a camera overlooking the street to see him getting out of his car, another by the door to see him stop for a photo-opportunity, another to watch him go up the stairs (one at a time), another on the landing to see him pass beneath the sign saying 'Admin Red Hall' and another to see him go through into the sports hall itself. He waved, he smiled, he said nothing. The feeling in the studio was that he looked confident, Cherie looked happy and young Euan would remember this night for a long time.

Nor was the appearance on screen of William Hague or Jack Straw sufficient to fill the vacuum, although we did have a fine cameo from Robin Cook, down the line from his Livingston count. When a querulous Paxman suggested that Labour was simply benefiting from Tory unpopularity, Cook replied: 'Jeremy, I think this is a time to be magnanimous. It would be churlish to deny the Conservative Party their part in our victory tonight.' Sir Marcus Fox, looking decidedly dicey in Shipley, was more mysterious than witty. What had gone wrong? 'Well, you don't have far to look, do you?' he said. 'I mean, it's the way in which the campaign was fought by our opponents, and they've pulled all their punches. The truth is we're all Thatcher children now, aren't we? The policies are being hijacked and the people somehow haven't been able to see it.'

In circumstances such as these, asking a psephologist for comment was akin to demanding the bowling figures before the cricket match has started, but that didn't stop Jonathan. 'Well, Jonathan,' Colin Rallings replied, groping for words, 'we're a little frustrated because we're waiting with bated breath for the marginals to come in.'

What about you, Alastair? 'Well I don't know what Colin's moaning about,' said Stewart. 'I've got the Battleground here and I can't fill any of it in yet.'

This could not go on, and mercifully it did not. The marginal seat of Birmingham Edgbaston was at last about to yield up its verdict.

Edgbaston is best known to the wider world as the home of a Test cricket ground and, to some, as the seat of Birmingham University. Much of the constituency is, to use the journalistic shorthand, 'leafy', which means that by normal English standards it is likely to vote Conservative. And so it has done since time immemorial. This was the seat of Neville Chamberlain and, more recently, of Jill Knight, whom Michael Brunson called 'the face of Tory womanhood'. Dame Jill held the seat with a majority of 4,000 at the 1992 election, and boundary changes since then were calculated to have added a further 1,000 to the Tory vote, giving a 'notional' majority of 5,000, but this had not prevented her from retiring. The new Conservative candidate, Andrew Marshall, arrived knowing that he had a battle on his hands for, despite its leafiness, Edgbaston presented distinct possibilities for Labour. The constituency points like a broad arrowhead towards the heart of Birmingham and at its thinner end has some distinctly Labour wards, while in the thicker, richer end sympathy towards Labour had grown. To win it in 1997, the Labour Party needed a swing of 5 per cent, which put Edgbaston at number 67 on its target list; that is to say, it was the 67th easiest (or least difficult) seat for Labour to win.

A little background on swings, as Alastair Stewart might have said. By normal standards, 5 per cent was an awful lot to ask. In 1945 Clement Attlee won with a huge national swing of 12 per cent, but since then Labour's best performance in terms of swing was 3 per cent in 1964, which got them elected by a whisker. This time, to win an overall majority, the *least* Labour needed nationally was 4.3 per cent. In other words, merely to take power by the slimmest of margins, Tony Blair had to produce the party's best showing in half a century and capture everything up to number 57 (Leeds North East) on his target list. If he was to have a working majority comparable to Mr Major's in 1992 – only just enough to last a five-year term – then Blair needed to win Edgbaston and a few more besides.

The votes from several Birmingham constituencies were being counted at the National Indoor Arena, but the count authorities there had decided to 'fast-track' two of them. These were Ladywood, safe seat of the plain person's heroine, Clare Short, and Edgbaston. It was this which put Edgbaston in position to be the first marginal to declare, making it the weathervane which would point the way the wind was blowing for the whole country. If Labour didn't win this seat, then it would probably not win a decent working majority. And remember, as yet there was no hard evidence to confirm that the much-courted voters in the marginals would back Labour as strongly as the voters in the handful of safe Labour seats seen to date.

Who, then, was carrying the flag for Labour in this contest? Gisela Stuart, 41, a law lecturer, who was in one important respect a very unlikely weathervane for British history. Stuart had been brought up on a farm 'in the middle of nowhere' in Bavaria, the daughter of a Czech mother and German father. She came to England at the age of 17 to learn the language and, despite finding herself in the middle of Ted Heath's three-day week, she liked the place and eventually settled. She took a degree in business studies, worked in publishing, married Mr Stuart, had two children, took another degree in law and became a lecturer at Birmingham University.

Gisela Stuart was a long-time Labour supporter and, as an expert on legal aspects of pensions, had advised the party on its response to Conservative pensions legislation. In 1994 she stood, unsuccessfully, in the elections for the European Parliament, and the following year she was chosen to fight Edgbaston. Although she regarded it as winnable, like most of the country she had doubts about actually winning. 'From the very first stages of sampling, 18 months ago, we seemed to be ahead, but whatever the figures told us we held back,' she recalls. Her campaign, in one of Labour's key targets, was well staffed and sophisticated, part of an attempt to sweep up south Birmingham, and the feeling of being part of such a big machine kept some of the pressure off her. 'Edgbaston is like a slice of middle England, with housing estates as well as the university and the middle-class areas. I always felt that if we as the Labour Party didn't take this seat then we were not going to win nationally. So it wasn't a personal matter; it was bigger than just me.'

The canvass figures always favoured her, as did some less scientific yardsticks. 'Jeff Rooker [a veteran Birmingham MP] has a theory that if the kids on the street aren't calling you names, then you must be doing all right. Well, in Edgbaston the kids were following us around saying they would vote Labour if they could. That seemed a pretty good sign.' The campaign itself, however, had its ugly moments, with several attempts to make an issue of her German background. There were reports of voters being urged to Keep Edgbaston British, but, Stuart says, 'the returns were rock solid'.

When the polls closed at 10 p.m. she already knew that Edgbaston would be an early declarer and that, win or lose, she would be in the national spotlight. She slipped into 'mental neutral'. 'I can do that. I say to myself that the only way is forward, and I just carry on. It's only after the event that I feel nervous and ask, "How did I do that?"' She killed a little time. 'I had a shower, I sat down and listened to the radio. Then I went to the count, arriving at about 11.15 p.m.' Another hour passed before the declaration, but she was not kept on tenterhooks, for her staff were able to tell her the result much earlier.

At nineteen minutes past midnight, with the nation watching, the returning officer began to speak. There were five candidates, and Stuart was the last in alphabetical order. Each name brought up a small cheer, but when we reached 'Gisela Stuart, the Labour Party candidate, twenty-three thousand . . .' the crowd erupted. And not just there. The BBC cut to Trimdon Labour Club, probably typical of any Labour-supporting crowd watching anywhere in the country, and found the members on their feet in front of their screens, waving, cheering and stamping. In Birmingham, Stuart's own face was a picture of delight.

She had turned the constituency on its head, converting a Conservative majority of 5,000 into a Labour majority of the same size. The swing was a whisker short of 10 per cent, twice what she needed and enough to lend some credibility at last to all those studio predictions. Laughing, she stepped forward and spoke from notes in her clipped and accented English. 'I'd like to thank the people of Edgbaston for entrusting me with being their first ever Labour Member of Parliament. Britain has turned away from the Tories, but this is not a time to look back. Today we look forward.' She spoke of one nation, of making Britain better and of Tony Blair, and she concluded: 'We will look back on May the 1st, 1997 as the day education became Britain's first priority, as the day we started a real attack on unemployment, and as the day the NHS was saved.'

At last we had our Basildon for 1997, and a jubilant new face to go with it. And this result was symbolic in more ways than one, for Gisela Stuart was the first Labour woman to be elected who had been chosen as a candidate from an all-women shortlist, and if her swing was matched elsewhere there would be dozens more like her. It was the culmination of what had been a painful process for Labour, as the leadership's decision to require a proportion of winnable constituencies to pick women had been

6. Gisela Stuart (left) and Clare Short celebrate in Birmingham.

bitterly opposed, and was ultimately (although too late for many men) declared illegal. Tony Blair had accepted that it would be a one-off, employed on this single occasion to force open the door of Westminster to women MPs.

But if Edgbaston goes down in history as the watershed result of 1997 it may be a small injustice, for the truth is that it was *not* the first seat to change hands from Conservative to Labour. It was the first seat to change hands *live on television*. A hundred miles away on the northern outskirts of Liverpool the constituency of Crosby got there 15 minutes earlier, but nobody planning the TV coverage had realized Crosby was a marginal, and you can hardly blame them. Even leafier than Edgbaston, it stood way down at number 120 on Labour's target list. A huge swing of 10 per cent was required to overturn the majority of 9,500 held by the sitting Tory, Sir Malcolm Thornton, who was standing again. No need to keep an eye on that one, or so it had seemed.

Well, Clare Curtis-Thomas, an engineer and academic aged 39, won Crosby for Labour and won it handsomely, ending up with more than half of the vote and a majority of 7,000. What is more, the figures were even juicier than Edgbaston's. The swing was an astonishing 18 per cent, far higher than the national exit poll predictions and almost double Gisela Stuart's; and the victory had been assisted by a remarkable collapse in the Liberal Democrat vote. Crosby had once, briefly, been an SDP seat for Shirley Williams, but now the well-heeled LibDems of Crosby were voting tactically in their thousands to get the Conservatives out. To their credit, ITV had spotted the upset and reported it as a Labour gain before the Edgbaston result, but they did not know the size of the swing, nor were they able to show the declaration live, so it was Gisela Stuart and not Clare Curtis-Thomas who was given a place in electoral folklore.

Minutes later there was another result and another little piece of history as Labour captured Portsmouth North from the Conservatives. This was more notable as a defeat than as a victory, for it marked the end of the political career of Peter Griffiths, a man who for a brief moment had been nationally famous, way back in 1964. Griffiths entered the Commons in that year after defeating Patrick Gordon Walker, Labour's Foreign Secretary-designate, in a notorious campaign in the Midlands seat of Smethwick in which voters there were allegedly told: 'If you want a nigger for a neighbour, vote Labour.' Shortly afterwards Harold Wilson caused a sensation during the Queen's Speech debate when he described Griffiths as a 'parliamentary leper' and dared the Tories to disown him. Griffiths lost Smethwick in 1966, but he returned to parliament eventually in 1979 when he won the Portsmouth seat, and since then had served quietly, if without distinction or preferment. Now he was out, replaced by Syd Rapson, 55, a former aircraft fitter and more recently leader of

Portsmouth city council. Rapson had needed a swing of 9 per cent to win, and he ended up with 14 per cent and a majority of 4,000.

With swings of 14 and even 18 per cent bringing them constituencies which were not even among their 90 key targets, Labour was now looking at something truly extraordinary. But they were not alone, for the Liberal Democrats too were at last beginning to see a breakthrough.

To be a Liberal in twentieth-century Britain is to know the taste of disappointment at its bitterest. It is like supporting Wales at rugby union these days, but without any good old days to be nostalgic about. The Liberals last enjoyed an overall majority in parliament under Asquith, and from 1945 to 1979 their highest total of seats was the 14 captured in the heyday of Jeremy Thorpe, of unhappy memory. The Liberal–SDP Alliance, despite a huge national vote, managed only 23 seats in 1983 and one fewer in 1987, and the 1992 election wiped out a string of by-election gains to dump the Liberal Democrats back on 20. Almost worse than all these feeble national showings was the long string of near misses in target constituencies, which in 1992 included Brecon and Radnorshire, lost to the Tories by 130 votes, and Portsmouth South, lost by 242. This party, it seemed, would never get the rub of the green.

From the very first minutes after polling closed, however, Paddy Ashdown had spoken of his confidence, and the party's headquarters for the night, at the Pizza on the Park Restaurant in central London, was abuzz. The exit polls showed the Liberal Democrats winning 18 per cent of the vote, exactly the same figure as in 1992; for once, however, it seemed that the complex mathematics of third-party politics were favourable and seats were set to fall. ITV was predicting a final tally of 45, and no one at the Pizza on the Park was arguing with that. Yet they needed iron stomachs, and it had nothing to do with the pizzas.

The earliest results showed the LibDem vote falling again and again in those safe Labour seats, and after midnight there was a run of setbacks. Birmingham Yardley was a three-way marginal in which the LibDems, Labour and the Tories were all in with a chance, and the LibDems had concentrated a good deal of their West Midlands effort there. But Labour held on comfortably. Then came Oldham East and Saddleworth. This, after some boundary tinkering, was the successor seat to Littleborough and Saddleworth, scene of the acrimonious 'Little and Sad' by-election in 1995. That was won by the LibDem Chris Davies, but early reports now suggested that Davies had lost it to the man he had narrowly beaten in 1995, Labour's Phil Woolas. Worse still, the word from Rochdale suggested that LibDem frontbencher Liz Lynne was in deep trouble against Labour in what had once been the stronghold of Cyril Smith. Three down: was it all going wrong again?

The answer was: no. Before long the Liberal Democrats had made three important gains from the Conservatives, and Ashdown's confidence was at last looking justified. Each victory now was as sweet as past defeats had been bitter. First there was Southport. The declaration was read by a solid-looking burgher in what Frank Skinner would call a necklace, and behind him was a placard saying 'Southport: eminently special' in a squiggly script doubtless intended to communicate the resort's refinement. There on the platform, to the right of the returning officer, stood Ronnie Fearn, the marathon man of Liberal politics.

Fearn first stood for this constituency in the election of February 1974, the year in which he became a local councillor. At that time it was a Conservative stronghold, and so it remained. Fearn, a local man and a bank clerk, stood again in October 1974, and in 1979, and in 1983, and still he failed. In 1987, however, the long-serving Tory MP, Sir Ian Percival, retired, and at his fifth attempt Fearn finally won the seat. Some thought that Southport had acquired its own Cyril Smith, but it was not to be. In 1992 the voters turned Tory again and at the age of 61 Fearn was out. Now, in 1997 the LibDems' most indomitable candidate was back for another try. 'Ronald Cyril Fearn, Liberal Democrat,' said the man in the chain, 'twenty-four thousand, three hundred and forty-six.' There was a modest cheer and a small smile. 'I hereby declare that Ronald Cyril Fearn has been duly elected.' Fearn's majority was 6,000 and the swing from the Conservatives had been a very solid 9 per cent.

It was soon apparent that this was no statistical blip, for Portsmouth, which had already given Labour a gain, now handed one to the LibDems. The seat of Portsmouth South, probably more than any other in the country, epitomized the pain of Liberal Democrat existence. Way back in 1984 Mike Hancock won it for the SDP–Liberal Alliance in a by-election, and then lost it three years later by a miserable 205 votes. Hancock stood again in 1992, only to lose again, this time by 242 votes. Rarely can the electoral fates have been crueller, but Hancock is made of that same stuff which kept Ronnie Fearn going through seven campaigns, so here he was again in 1997. On a very low turnout of 64 per cent he actually polled fewer votes than last time, but it was more than enough, for the Conservative vote had collapsed and Hancock was back in parliament with a majority of 4,000.

And there was more. In 1992 the LibDem Andrew Stunell had failed to take the Manchester seat of Hazel Grove by just 929 votes, but now the name of Hazel Grove popped up on the ITV screen marked 'LD gain' – on a swing of 13 per cent, Stunell now held it by a thumping margin of 12,000 votes. With reports from Sheffield suggesting that another huge swing there would hand them the well-heeled Hallam constituency, the Liberal Democrats in London were starting to order extra topping on their pizzas.

Paddy Ashdown, having swapped his orange sweater for a suit and tie, was heading for the Yeovil count with his wife Jane when he gave his reaction. There were commiserations for Liz Lynne and Chris Davies – 'They'll be back' – and quiet pride over Southport and Hallam. As he spoke, word reached him of the Portsmouth South result, but the most he would do was express his satisfaction for Mike Hancock (it was Mrs Ashdown's face that betrayed delight). This was control, restraint. He can have been in no doubt that this was a historic occasion for his party, the first election night in decades which they could greet without disappointment, but he was saving his jubilation for later. Perhaps, as a Somerset MP, he wanted to see the south-west painted yellow first.

Elsewhere, the people were deciding with a vengeance. Although famously it had not fallen to Labour in 1992, Basildon had come within 1,500 votes of doing so. The boundary commissioners, in adjusting the shape of the constituency, had since then thrown in another 1,000 Tory voters, but David Amess, the Conservative hero of that night, seeing how tenuous his grip was, had switched to the safer seat of Southend West. Target number 29 and needing just a 2 per cent swing, Basildon was firmly in Labour's sights. Yet victory there, however confidently expected, would always be an important moment, even an exorcism.

Just how badly the party was scarred by that 1992 defeat could be measured from a Labour training video for canvassers issued in 1996. *Target to Talk* opened with the words, 'You may find these scenes distressing,' and then replayed the footage of the 1992 Basildon declaration. Before the returning officer even spoke, a beaming Amess could be seen embracing his wife, and once the vital number had been read out he threw both arms skywards in a victory gesture seared for ever in Labour minds. From this scene the Labour video cut suddenly to Tony Blair: 'You remember how we felt on the day after that last election? Well we never want to feel that way again.' At twelve minutes before 1 a.m. the Basildon ghost was finally laid and a stake driven through its heart. Labour's Angela Smith, a red-headed Essex woman of 38, crushed the Conservative with a swing of 15 per cent to win a majority of 13,000. 'In Basildon, and in Britain, Labour has come home,' she declared.

Minutes later it had come home in Norwich North, until 1983 a Labour fastness but since then a Tory-held marginal. Like Basildon, it was marginal no longer, an 11 per cent swing giving Labour's Ian Gibson a comfortable majority of 9,000. And Labour was also claiming some notable scalps. In the south London district of Battersea, junior health minister John Bowis suffered the peculiarly bitter blow, for a Tory, of being defeated by a *Guardian* journalist, Martin Linton (the man, incidentally, who had edited his newspaper's hefty election guide). And in Wolverhampton South West, held long ago by Enoch Powell and since then the domain of Nicholas Budgen, Labour's Jenny Jones took over easily. 'This is a wonderful result, it really is,' she declared, with emotion in her voice. 'It's beyond my wildest dreams.' Budgen had spent his 23 years in parliament on the back benches but became well known nationally because of his relentless Euro-scepticism; he was one of the eight rebels kicked out of the parliamentary party for five months in 1994. Among that group he was regarded as one of the least batty; indeed, put-downs from this wry and wiry man were more than many Tory frontbenchers could cope with. Now they need fear him no longer.

*

David Dimbleby, meanwhile, had the wind at his back, literally. We glimpsed his big E-desk over his shoulder and saw that he had no fewer than five TV screens sunk into it before him. It may have been to keep these ventilated, and it may have been the explanation for his own steady cool, but a breeze was clearly playing across this scene because every time we saw David he was holding down the fluttering pages of his notebooks like a mariner on deck with his charts. That's the sort of problem which rehearsals are supposed to sort out. Across the studio, Peter Snow was also having trouble, but this was a difficulty no one could have anticipated. His swingometer wasn't really big enough. Snow fed in the results from Edgbaston, Portsmouth North and Crosby and clicked the little switch in his left hand. Starting again from the zero line, vertically downwards, the arrow dutifully swung up and left into blue Tory territory. 'This is what's going to happen in these vital seats if these three are typical: something like 12 per cent,' said our man, sweeping his hand across a forest of little red figures representing Labour gains. But that might not be the limit. 'In *Crosby*, the furthest one, here, it was *eighteen* per cent.' But the arrow didn't move. Instead, Snow had to gesticulate towards the top left-hand corner of his big screen and declare: 'It's off the end here somewhere.'

By now Snow was allowed to make specific forecasts. Influenced by the exit poll fiasco of 1992, the BBC had taken the decision not to predict the number of seats each party was likely to win until sufficient results were in to compute from. It had thus been deliberately vague for two and a half hours, quoting only the vote percentage given in the exit poll and leaving Snow's swingometer to indicate rough numbers – more than 100, around 150, less than 200, and so on. But once a couple of dozen real results had landed, Snow began to be specific, and every time he gave a figure for Labour's likely majority it seemed to go up. He started on 171 but soon quoted 193 and even for a moment 203. Clicking up his Battleground graphic, which showed plenty of red and yellow blobs coming in but still not a single blue, he declared it a 'terrifying sight for the Conservatives'.

On ITV Alastair Stewart was also excited. 'Jonathan,' he announced portentously, 'the only thing that's going to be the same about the House of Commons is the architecture. Everything else has changed tonight, and changed radically.' And then he did the holodeck thing. 'Let's bring it in, here into the studio: the Speaker's chair behind me, government benches to the right, opposition benches to the left.' And presto! there it was again, all that green leather. Next: 'Bring in the MPs and colour them according to their party affiliations.' Rows of men in suits filled the benches, and the great majority of them turned red. Stewart gave the figures: Labour 410, Conservatives 177, Liberal Democrats 44 and others 28. 'Crunch it all together and our prediction is that Mr Blair will be looking at a majority of . . . 161. Edging up, Jonathan.'

The BBC may not have had the holodeck, but it did have an interview with Tony Blair's press secretary. This was a coup, an event in its own right, for Alastair Campbell, though his best friend would not describe him as shy, tends to avoid speaking on camera. John Simpson introduced him for an 'informal chat' (clearly a negotiated formula) and Campbell underlined this informality by declining to look anywhere near the camera. After all those politicians and others giving us the full frontal, the effect was disconcerting. Simpson, catching his eye, asked how things were going.

'I think we're having a pretty good night.'

What about a majority of 171?

'I would doubt that, but it's fair to say we've had a very good campaign and we're having a very good night,' he said flatly.

Gazing intently at Simpson's right ear, Campbell stonewalled in this downbeat fashion until at last a thought occurred which suddenly animated him. The long campaign, he said, had rebounded against the Tories. 'I think we had a great campaign at every level. I think Tony was on great form, John Prescott had a brilliant campaign, Gordon Brown running things from Millbank, the whole Millbank Tower operation under Peter Mandelson, and the integration of the Shadow Cabinet as well. And I think really important is our organization on the ground. We have got a fantastic organization on the ground now and the truth is that we have supplanted the Conservatives as the professional party in British politics.'

At London's Festival Hall, where Labour's big party was getting under way, another unexpected interviewee was saying his piece. If Tony Blair had had one little frustration throughout the campaign, it was his failure to secure a formal endorsement from Richard Branson. In order to reassure the moneyed classes, Blair had wanted backing from reputable businessmen; Branson, who is the personification of the business winner, was the top target. Blair met him more than once, but somehow they did not team up.

Branson, as the police would say, had previous in politics, having been involved in one of Margaret Thatcher's most eccentric stunts. Returning from a foreign trip while still Prime Minister, Thatcher had been disgusted by the dirty state of London's streets, so she summoned the press to a patch of lawn by the Palace of Westminster for an important event. When she appeared she was armed with plastic bag and spike, and for the benefit of the cameras she picked up some artfully arranged rubbish. This was, it was announced, the start of an anti-litter crusade, and to lead it she recruited someone who she presumably thought would command the respect of the littering classes: Richard Branson.

The crusade was soon forgotten, but it highlighted Branson's debt to Thatcher, whose tax and deregulation policies had multiplied his fortune. Something, however, went wrong under John Major: Branson did not win the licence to operate the National Lottery, a defeat which smarted all the more since he had offered to run it without profit, and he was obliged to wait a surprisingly long time to be awarded a railway line of his own. Yet despite his disillusionment, Branson refused to switch sides and endorse New Labour.

So it was an unusual decision by Blair to invite the Virgin boss to his party's party, and an unusual decision by Branson to turn up among the first guests. Tories among his admiring customers would surely think him a turncoat and an ingrate, while Labour supporters might think an endorsement that *followed* an election victory smacked of opportunism. As the BBC's Francine Stock pluckily put it to him, after sitting on the fence throughout the campaign he had 'jumped off it pretty smartly this evening'. Branson appeared to blush. 'Well, I still haven't declared who I voted for, but I think Labour have many policies which we've come out and said we do support. Tonight's an historic night and they've been good enough to invite us and some other people down, and we're here to wish them well and I hope that they have a very successful five years in office. And I think they need all the support they can get.'

All this was said less assertively than it appears on the page, for Branson is an awkward performer on television. He went on, however, to identify some things Labour had got right – 'issues like health, trying to stop kids from starting to smoke, trying to direct some of the lottery money to health and education'. As for Blair, 'the area where he can win through is making decisions with slightly more of a heart than perhaps the Tories did in the past'. A little later he gave ITV an even better soundbite: 'What

53

they [Labour] have said is that they will take all the best Tory policies forward and that they will refine some of those policies.'

Even without the Branson endorsement, Blair's party was doing rather well. After thirty-odd results, patterns were emerging, most of all the pattern which the experts had predicted but which nobody had ever seen before. The swings in the marginals *were* greater than the swings in safer seats, which was part of the reason for the swingometer's problems. Perhaps 8, 9 and 10 per cent in solid Labour constituencies, but 12, 15 and even 18 per cent in Tory-held marginals. This meant that Labour was reaching into areas it had never touched before, capturing the 'leafy' suburban vote in Birmingham Edgbaston, Birmingham Hall Green, and Crosby on the edge of Liverpool. And where Labour was not sweeping up the leafies, the LibDems were: in Hazel Grove, Manchester, and Hallam, Sheffield. The Tories had lost both seats in Portsmouth. As Michael Brunson was quick to point out, they were being driven out of the great cities of the land, and Battersea, that first London declaration, was an ill omen for them in the capital. Kenneth Clarke, the Chancellor of the Exchequer, was the first of the party's big hitters to put his hands up. 'It looks as though we've lost,' he said.

CHAPTER FOUR

1 a.m. to 2 a.m.

The Sedgefield candidate – an inspirational speech –
Hunt and Fox – 'Con hold' at last – venom in Putney –
Cabinet casualty – a Muslim MP – golden dawn for
LibDems – Ashdown's unspoken words –
Labour tide – Hove? – Nintendo moment – Celtic
backlash – calling Redwood.

It has been said of the partnership between Tony Blair and his constituency of Sedgefield that it is a marriage made in heaven. That may be so, but there is no denying that they married in haste. Sedgefield is leafy, although not in the sense in which metropolitan journalists use the word. It is a slice of rural County Durham where, deep underground beneath the trees, fields and villages, men used to cut coal. They don't do it any more, and the countryside today is unstained by pitheads or their attendant industry, but the people have not lost their habit of voting Labour.

In a sense, like Blair the Oxford Christian, Sedgefield was born again. The constituency, sprawling across the county north of Darlington, was abolished in 1974 by the boundary commissioners and then re-created in 1983. When the election of that year was called, it had no sitting MP and no chosen candidate and, since this was a time when winnable Labour seats were at something of a premium, applications flooded in.

Tony Blair, then just 30, was far from being the obvious choice. He was a bright young thing who had done his bit by fighting a by-election in a hopeless seat (losing his deposit) and he was obviously bursting with ambition. Also on the plus side, he had been brought up in Durham. On the minus side, however, he was the son of a Tory barrister who had been sent to a posh school in Scotland and then to Oxford, after which he had worked as a lawyer in London. How the Sedgefield Labour Party ended up picking him is already the stuff of legend. He hustled. He made some very useful friends in the Trimdon branch, notably the branch secretary, John Burton. And he got his name shoe-horned on to the shortlist at the last minute. Then, thanks to his charm, some smart manoeuvring and the support of the 'Trimdon posse', he became the candidate. You can tell what a coup this was by looking at the list of his disappointed rivals, who included Joel Barnett, the former Cabinet Minister, Sid Weighell, the rail union boss, and Ben Pimlott, the historian. It says something about the Labour Party of the time that it was none of these, but the left-winger, Les Huckfield, who provided the stiffest opposition. Once Blair was the candidate there was no question of losing in the election, and three weeks later he duly entered parliament with a majority of 8,000.

This association with Sedgefield proved so fruitful over the years that Blair was to portray the seat as a model for the new Labour Party he wanted to create. The biggest change was in the membership, for Blair, Burton and others set about enlisting new members with all the zeal of Mormon missionaries, offering special rates, luring in whole families and recruiting as individual members trade unionists who were already paying the levy. Blair's biographer, John Rentoul, writes that within a year Sedgefield Labour Party was having barbecues instead of branch meetings, and the sharp-eyed John Smith was describing it as 'a brown ale and claret constituency'. A much broader membership gave it broader-minded politics – Blair was, as he put it, giving the party back to the people it represented.

Fourteen years on from that first arrival at Sedgefield, after a triumphant progress from his home in Trimdon to the count at Newton Aycliffe Leisure Centre, Tony Blair joined the line-up in the glare of the television lights to hear his fourth declaration in the constituency. Looking as nervous as a first-timer, he reached out to take the hand of his wife, Cherie Booth. Behind her, scribbling notes, stood John Burton, and strung out on Blair's left were the candidates from the Conservative, Liberal Democrat, Referendum and Socialist Labour parties. As the returning officer began to speak, a hush descended.

Anthony Charles Lynton Blair received 33,500 votes, or 71 per cent of all those cast, and he emerged with a majority of 25,000 over the Conservative, Elizabeth Pitman. He nodded and smiled uneasily to acknowledge the applause and then, at the words 'has been duly elected . . .' he kissed his wife, shook the losers by the hand and moved to the podium. Though the smile was broad the eyes, flicking to left and right, betrayed his unease: someone had trodden on his grave. But when he began to speak he grew visibly more comfortable. He thanked the returning officer, the police, the counters and the leisure centre staff. He thanked the other candidates: 'I'm sorry they haven't seen as much of me as perhaps they would have liked – or perhaps not. I know that it has been a very clean and a very good campaign, and if I can say this to Lizzie, who came second and is the Conservative candidate: I once fought a very hopeless Conservative seat in Beaconsfield in the south of England, and look what happened to me. So you never can tell.' He thanked the 'absolutely magnificent' voters of Sedgefield. 'The greatest pleasure I have is to serve you with all my heart and with all my energy.'

Next came some personal remarks. 'Perhaps you will allow me to say a word of thanks in particular to my family, who are here this evening. To Cherie, who has been such a wonderful source of strength to me all through the last few weeks, indeed all through my political life. And all my family, who are here. If I could say a special word of welcome to my father, who was with me when I was first elected in 1983, and who has just been magnificent to me all my life. I would never, ever have done what I have done without him. I know that for him, like me, all that could have made this moment complete was that my mother was here as well.' His voice faltered slightly, but he moved quickly on. 'I would like to thank, too, all Cherie's family [her father, the actor Tony Booth, was in the crowd] for their strength and support, and of course all my good and loyal party workers, not least my agent, John Burton, who is a star in his own right [cheers and applause].'

This was unscripted, palpably heartfelt and generous. With the nation watching, Blair might have been tempted to rush through the words of thanks to reach his general remarks, but instead he was taking his time as he moved from the personal and local towards the national. 'If I can just say this to you all: it is an honour to serve you, and I feel this evening a deep sense of honour, a deep sense of responsibility and a deep sense of humility. You have put your trust in me, and I intend to repay that trust. I will not let you down. When I think back over the last 14 years that I have been a Member of Parliament for this constituency, it is an area that has undergone the most dramatic and extraordinary change, and all through those difficult changes there has been a spirit in this constituency and in the community surrounding it, and that spirit has been the spirit of unity, of determination to take on the challenge of change and overcome it, and work for the good of all the people of this constituency. And that is actually the spirit that our country needs now. Because if we have been as successful as the indications are that we have been – and you know me, all the way through I've been against complacency and I'm still against it until those results finally come through – if we have done well, then I know what this is a vote for. It is a vote for the future. It is not a vote for outdated dogma or ideology of any kind. It is a vote for an end to divisions, an end to looking backwards, a desire to apply the basic, decent British values of common sense and imagination to the problems we all know we face as a country today. And it is with a real sense of pride that we have created a Labour Party today capable of offering that unity of purpose, that vision of renewal that our country needs. So that with those decent values in place we can tackle the problems that our country faces. In our schools, in our hospitals, the crime on our streets, the jobs for our young people, the industries for the future – the very basic things that determine whether a country succeeds or fails. We are a great country; the British people are a great people. There is no greater honour than to serve them, and serve them we will. Thank you.'

Politicians these days are rarely given five uninterrupted minutes to speak to so large an audience, and when they do the performance is usually scripted, rehearsed and packaged. This was something quite different, and it was all the more refreshing and moving for it. Even Peter Mandelson, who had watched in nearby Hartlepool, was choked. 'All my adult life I have been waiting and working for this moment, and to see such an inspirational speech from such a great man as Tony Blair fills me with enormous pride, and such pleasure that I can hardly describe.' The Labour leader was four days short of his 44th birthday and, as Peter Snow explained, about to become the youngest British prime minister since Lord Liverpool in 1812. The scenes that followed his speech only underlined his youth, for he stepped from the platform and picked up his daughter for a cuddle and a chat, then ruffled the heads of his two sons. There would soon be children in Downing Street, and they would not be the PM's grandchildren.

Across the country momentous changes were happening. Sir Marcus Fox, who had never figured in the Dicey Dozen, was defeated in Shipley. An MP for 27 years and, as chairman of the 1922 Committee, one of the most influential of all Conservatives, Sir Marcus had never dreamt that his 12,000 majority could be swept away. The swing was 14 per cent and the winner was Christopher Leslie, a local boy born two years after Sir Marcus had entered the Commons. As the Fox departed, so did the Hunt. In Wirral West, David Hunt, who for five years had been a Cabinet Minister under John Major before slipping from favour, was defeated by another 14 per cent swing. And in Upminster, on the eastern edge of London, Foreign Office Minister Sir Nicholas Bonsor was removed by a 15 per cent swing. It was beginning to look as though there was no such thing as a safe Conservative seat anywhere. Wirral West, after all, was Labour target number 131, Shipley was number 133 and Upminster was 144. Peter Snow had to reassure us that the Conservatives would eventually win *some* seats.

The Tories had been kept waiting because their shire heartlands were precisely the areas where the counts were delayed by the local elections, but now at last, a few minutes after Tony Blair had spoken, the words 'Con hold' flashed on the screen. Cecil Parkinson, the fertilizer man who was proving such a welcome alternative to all those posturing ministers, was talking to Paxman. Upon learning of his party's first victory, Cecil rose to the moment. 'I'm very relieved,' he announced. 'I was actually beginning to think that John Major [holder of the safest Tory seat in the country] would remain leader of the party and the only member we had in the House of Commons.' Beside him, Neil Kinnock and Sir David Steel could be seen laughing merrily.

When, moments later, Paxman brought the 'terribly good news' of a second Tory win, Parkinson replied: 'Very good, so we're going to have a rival for the leadership.' From this we switched abruptly to the declaration at Putney.

Whatever happened in this socially mixed constituency on the south bank of the Thames, it was bound to make headlines. In the first place it was the seat of David Mellor, whose abrasiveness and thirst for publicity alone would have ensured him fame, without any unplanned dramas to help. A Major loyalist, he had been rewarded in 1992 with his dream job, as the National Heritage Minister who would in due course become the bountiful distributor of lottery millions. Within months, however, his private life was all over the newspapers. He had had an affair with an actress, Antonia de Sancha, whose 'friends' paraded through the papers a succession of lurid stories (toe-sucking, sex in a Chelsea strip) which left the Minister, for all his denials, looking ridiculous.

Weeks later he was in trouble again, as one of *his* friends, Mona Bauwens, revealed during a libel case (in which he was not directly involved) that the Mellor family had enjoyed a month's holiday with her in Marbella, largely at her expense. She had booked and paid for the flights and had paid for the rent of the villa. This was criticized in the Press, and Mellor resigned. But although he was out, he was not down – indeed, we seemed suddenly to see and hear even more of him, often as a journalist and commentator on sport, sometimes as an unofficial apologist for the government and sometimes as one of those celebs who get on television simply because we love to hate them. Among those who loved to hate him most, it turned out, was Sir James Goldsmith.

Sir James, ploughing a reported £20 million into his

Referendum Party campaign to bully the Conservatives into Euro-scepticism (or, failing that, into opposition), chose to make his own personal stand against Mellor in Putney. Mellor's response – he talks in tabloid headlines, all pith and outrage – was predictably venomous, and Putney became a needle match. A good measure of national interest in a particular constituency contest is the number of fringe candidates it attracts, and Putney had half a dozen, including representatives of the Renaissance Democrats, the Freedom to Party Party and the Independent Beautiful Party. There was also a Sportsmen's Alliance / Anything-But-Mellor candidate, testimony to Mellor's aggressive advocacy, following the Dunblane massacre, of the banning of handguns.

Almost forgotten in all this was Labour's Tony Colman. A wealthy former businessman (once a senior figure at Burtons), Colman had spent the past six years as leader of Merton council. He had stood for parliament once before, unsuccessfully, in 1979, and was persuaded to return to the fray this time because he was sure Labour was going to win the election and that Putney would be carried by the tide. 'It's one of those seats that, when you get a change of government, it changes too.' His confidence was not widely shared. Needing an 8 per cent swing, Putney stood at the outer limit of Labour's 90 target seats and was generally thought to be safe for Mellor because of his strong local following. Although the Labour campaign went well, by polling day Colman was beginning to think the doubters might be right. 'I wasn't confident. Mellor was issuing a new leaflet every night and I thought it might have an effect. I just couldn't tell whether I would squeak home.'

A forgotten security pass delayed Colman's arrival at the count and, once there, he searched frantically for a TV to hear the exit polls. Like so many others, however, when he saw them he didn't believe them, and this scepticism seemed justified a little later when one of his supporters told him firmly that he had lost. Crestfallen, he gazed blankly at the count, assuming it was all over and reconciling himself to defeat. Only in the final moments of counting did he notice with some surprise that his bundles of votes were beginning to overhaul Mellor's.

Minutes later, after the customary huddle with the returning officer, the candidates trooped on to the platform, Colman on the way exchanging his very first words with Sir James Goldsmith ('Good evening.' 'Good evening.'). Mellor, looking uncharacteristically glum and uncomfortable, nevertheless positioned himself at centre stage to hear the result, with Colman tucked in behind. Labour won by 3,000 votes on a swing of 11 per cent. Goldsmith polled 1,500, not enough to have made a difference to the outcome, and lost his deposit. The pro-handgun campaigner got 100 votes and the Renaissance Democrat, who had argued that British politics lacked poetry, marked up an achievement of sorts with just 7. David Mellor had been defeated, and there was some jeering from the floor.

The television producers quickly cut away to studio analysis and other results, but this was a mistake. Unwatched by the nation, Colman made a magnanimous speech of acceptance, ending with a generous tribute to the Tory loser. At this there were more growls from the floor, which continued as Mellor himself stepped to the microphone. He began with a kind remark about Colman and the Liberal Democrat, and then, turning to the rest of the candidates, he let rip. All his years as a fellow of the Royal Zoological Society, he declared, had not prepared him for such a collection. At this the growling turned to a roar of 'Out! Out! Out!' and a slow handclap, but Mellor continued to slosh petrol on the flames. Sir James, he declared, 'has got nothing to be smug about. And I would like to say that 1,500 votes is a derisory total and we have shown tonight that the Referendum

Party is dead in the water.' The billionaire and a few others on the platform, just a few feet from the speaker, joined in the chanting and clapping. It made an ugly and memorable spectacle. Mellor raised his voice above the din to deliver one last insult: 'And Sir James, you can get off back to Mexico knowing your attempt to buy the British political system has failed.'

By now the television cameras were on again, but they had missed some of the excitement and the effect was curiously distorting. Sir James and his friends were shown behaving like a bunch of Brownshirts and Mellor's final remarks appeared a perfectly justified response. Jonathan Dimbleby spoke of 'the most extraordinary violation of the normal rules of democratic behaviour', while his brother David offered the cooler 'rather wild scenes at Putney'. What neither Dimbleby had seen was

7. David Mellor in Putney, jeered by Sir James Goldsmith.

Mellor's provocative crack about the Royal Zoological Society, which might have led them to a different view of the affair.

Mellor, appearing on both channels in quick succession, had his tail up, blaming the barracking on 'a small bunch of gun fanatics' and on Sir James, who had behaved 'as if he was boozed up at some rugby match'. He went on: 'We lost fair and square to the Labour Party tonight and I don't begrudge that . . . What I am very delighted has happened is that Goldsmith has been stopped dead in his tracks. His 1,500 votes is a derisory vote. I'm afraid that Putney has said, "Up your hacienda, Jimmy!"'

It was a fitting exit for Mellor, going down in a blaze of publicity and righteous indignation. Whether the Goldsmiths and the gun lobby – in all about 40 people – would have behaved quite so badly if he had spoken with more restraint we will never know. In any case it is not a question worth asking, for Mellor is incapable of that sort of restraint, and he himself had certainly been provoked enough during the campaign. What, the BBC asked him, would he do now that he was out of parliament? Moments such as this, he explained with a cheeky grin, showed how important it was for MPs to have outside interests to fall back on. He would be devoting himself full-time to his: 'You haven't – tragically – seen the last of me.'

In Scotland another household name was on the way out, and this time it was a Cabinet Minister. Michael Forsyth, the Scottish Secretary, had been at the front of the Dicey Dozen queue, and Peter Snow's cliff now fell on him. This time no one, not Forsyth himself, not Anne McGuire, the Labour candidate, and not the Scottish electorate, can have been surprised, for the seat of Stirling was sixth on Labour's target list. Forsyth had pulled off a dramatic escape in 1992, winning by 703 votes at a time when many had written him off. Since then the boundary commissioners had

65

trimmed that majority to a mere 250 votes. A swing of 0.28 per cent would tip the balance.

Forsyth was the man who brought the Stone of Scone back to Scotland on the eve of the election, the man who wore a kilt to the première of *Braveheart*, the man who coined the phrase 'Tartan Tax' and battered Labour with it relentlessly. He showed more flair and aggression than any other leading Conservative in taking the battle to the opposition, and Labour's discomfort and muddle over devolution were proof of his effectiveness. A dry-as-dust Thatcherite from a humble background, he was never quite at home in the genteel world of Scottish Conservatism, but his buccaneering ways at the Scottish Office since 1995 were thought to have given the party some hope.

It was not enough, however, to save him. He polled 14,000 votes, 2,000 fewer than in 1992, while McGuire, a former chair of the Scottish Labour Party, polled 20,000, up 4,000 on the 1992 score. She thus had a majority of more than 6,000 after a swing of 8 per cent. Forsyth was well and truly beaten, as he swiftly acknowledged. 'Reports of my political demise were not, in fact, exaggerated,' he declared. 'It's a good night for the Labour Party, there's no doubt about that. The only silver lining I could discover was that there were one or two members of the Scottish media who placed bets on me winning. I can take some consolation from that . . . It is a fact of politics that we live by the sword and we die by the sword.'

A lot of Scottish Conservatives were contemplating the sharp end of that sword. Although the swing to Labour in Stirling was smaller than in many English constituencies, the BBC's calculation was that the Tories would still lose eight seats north of the border and be left with just three: Eastwood, Gordon and North Tayside. 'When Anthony Eden was Prime Minister,' Snow reminded us, 'the Tories had half the seats in Scotland.' Eden's head duly appeared on Snow's big screen with a tower upon it topped by the number 36. Next came Ted Heath's head with a smaller tower and 20, and Thatcher's in 1987, with 10 Scottish seats. This rose to 11 in 1992, when Major 'managed to bump it up one'. 'But now,' said Snow, 'we are forecasting that John Major's Conservative Party will be down to an all-time low of' – the words came out staccato – '*three . . . seats . . . in . . . Scotland.*'

While the Conservatives suffered, 'Mr Buchan' also met a setback. Alex Salmond of the SNP had said that Glasgow Govan was 'on a knife edge', but when it came off that edge it was on Labour's side, amid unpleasant scenes. This was a seat that had twice been captured in by-elections by the SNP, and it represented easily their best hope of breaking into the huge Glasgow region. But the contest between Labour and the SNP in Govan was overshadowed by another contest within Labour itself. For a year the rival claims to the nomination of Mike Watson, a former Glasgow Central MP, and Mohammed Sarwar, a cash-and-carry millionaire, had split the local party. Two ballots were held, amid allegations of vote-rigging, and Sarwar had emerged victorious; but the affair left so much bitterness that the SNP had high hopes of overturning Labour's 5,000 majority. Their prospects seemed all the brighter when it emerged that, as the general election went ahead, the police were still investigating the vote fraud claims.

In such circumstances it was no surprise that the campaign was particularly bitter, and the presence of a British National Party candidate (Sarwar is originally from Pakistan) only aggravated this. The declaration itself was delayed when the other nine candidates refused to share a platform with the BNP man, Jim White, and some noisy barracking followed which led to police intervention. In the end Sarwar won by 3,000 votes, becoming Britain's first Muslim MP. Once again the SNP would have no Glasgow seats, and Labour's grip on the city was almost complete. But the SNP had compensation elsewhere as, despite some very unfavourable boundary changes, it held on to the Perth seat it had won in a 1995 by-election. Salmond was still set to make gains in the 1997 election.

The Liberal Democrats were on a roll. Having raised the yellow flag over Southport, Portsmouth South and Hazel Grove – all among their top targets – they learned of the scale of their victory in Sheffield Hallam. This seat was number 62 on their target list, but Richard Allan, a 31-year-old archaeologist from Bath, captured it with a swing of 18 per cent. And soon afterwards there was another unlikely triumph, this time in the Bristol area. Sir John Cope, a former Paymaster-General and Deputy Chairman of the Conservative Party, had sat for the seat of Northavon and its predecessor without a worry since 1974. His majority, allowing for boundary changes, was a steep 11,000, and even if you had added the Liberal Democrat and Labour votes together in 1992 he would still have won. But this time Sir John was in for a shock. The Conservative share of the vote collapsed from more than 50 per cent to less than 30 per cent, and Steven Webb, Professor of Social Studies at Bath University, won the seat for the LibDems by a margin of 2,000 votes on a 10 per cent swing.

Cheltenham and Bath, both taken from the Tories in 1992, were safely held by the LibDems, and Weston-super-Mare (target 20) was captured. In Torbay, where the Conservative Rupert Allason was defending a majority of 6,000, there was a recount and rumour had it that the gap between him and the LibDem was very close. On the evidence of advances such as these, predictions for the Liberal Democrats nationally had moved off the usual scale. ITV, which started by saying they would win 45 seats, adjusted to 55 and then to 57. The BBC briefly said 61, quickly corrected to 54 – 'levels not seen since Lloyd George' – and then 53. There was talk of gains in south-west London, scene in the past of some of the party's most agonizing near-misses, while observant viewers might have spotted on Peter Snow's big map that Folkestone and Hythe, seat of the Home Secretary, Michael Howard, was tipped to turn yellow.

Such glowing prospects were certain to cause as much anxiety as joy in the party of disappointment. To dare to hope was only to court heartbreak. They had won 20 seats in 1992, so 30 would have been a very good score this time. Surely they would lose some more of what they had? As Sir David Steel had pointed out to Paxman, the Labour tide seemed to be sweeping all before it, including LibDems such as Liz Lynne and Chris Davies. Surely, too, there would be the usual run of close seconds? Predictions of 55 and 61 seats seemed reckless and foolish. And yet look what had happened in Hallam and Northavon . . .

In this turmoil of emotions, Lord Holme, the LibDem campaign director, found a middling course: 'It's obviously an extremely good result, far beyond our expectations . . . I don't know where it will end, but I think with a parliamentary party twice the size we went into the election with.' That sounded like 45 or so. Would there be any more losses to Labour? 'I hope not. I think we've probably seen the worst of that, and most of the rest of the evening looks like the golden dawn we were talking about.'

Down in his own constituency of Yeovil, Paddy Ashdown took an easy win in his stride, looking calm and happy as he saw his majority rise by nearly 3,000 to 11,000. The seat he had fought and failed to win in 1979, and which he had captured riding the Alliance wave of 1983, was now very safe indeed. It was, he said, a privilege and an honour to serve the people of Yeovil, and he thanked all the usual people for the conduct of the election and count. 'I do not wish to predict the future,' he went on, 'but I will say this. We are now going to see a change of government and I believe there will be a very substantial, perhaps even a two-thirds majority, for constitutional change and the modernization of our system of government in the next parliament. I believe that can deliver a new era for our country, an era of politics which is more in touch with people, and an era where more power is in the hands of the voter and perhaps less in the hands of the political establishment and the elites, and I think that will be a very, very good thing for our democracy. For our part, we shall use the votes that are given to us tonight, in this constituency and elsewhere, where we have already made a number of gains, to make sure that in the next parliament we continue to fight for those things we have fought for during this campaign, above all for more investment in education, for more investment in the health service to tackle the crisis, and for a clear commitment to make sure that the constitution of our country is modernized to make our country ready for the next century. Thank you all very much indeed.'

Those ungainly words 'proportional representation' were never spoken, but they were present in every sentence of this speech, which was addressed as much to Tony Blair as to anyone else. Labour and the LibDems had agreed before the election on a common approach to the question of electoral reform, involving the establishment of a commission to decide on a new voting system and a referendum to follow. Ashdown was keen to highlight this, and for obvious reasons: in a proportional system, with 18 per cent of the vote, his party would be heading for 120 seats, not just 40 or 50. As he told ITV: 'Labour has made an agreement with us about how we might advance the cause of constitutional reform. I anticipate and believe that that agreement will be honoured. I do not believe that Mr Blair is a dishonourable man. He has made that agreement and I expect and believe that he will carry that forward.'

At this precise moment even the staunchest of PR enthusiasts in the Labour Party could have been forgiven for feeling some enthusiasm for the familiar first-past-the-post system, because up and down the land Labour candidates were turning out to be just that: first past the post. Ministers as well as the lowlier Tory lobby fodder just kept on hobbling in second. In Bolton West (target number 55) Tom Sackville, the junior Home Office Minister, was defeated. In Harwich (target 158) the Sports Minister, Ian Sproat, fell to a 15 per cent swing. Sproat, in fact, already knew the taste of defeat, having fallen victim back in 1983 to his own electoral miscalculation in Scotland. He had sat as member for marginal Aberdeen South for 13 years before deciding to switch to the promising country seat of Roxburgh and Berwickshire. Alas, he failed to win Roxburgh, while his Tory successor in Aberdeen, Gerry Malone, was returned safely in his place there. Now in 1997, five years after his return to parliament for Harwich, he had seen a majority of 15,000 votes vanish into thin air.

In Hornchurch (target 109), east of London, Education Minister Robin Squire bit the dust, losing the seat on a 16 per cent swing to John Cryer. This, if you have the patience, is the first link in a curious chain of connections. Cryer's mother, Ann Cryer, had also been elected, a few minutes earlier, for Keighley (43), and she was the widow of a former Keighley MP, Bob Cryer, who was killed in a road accident in 1994. Mrs Cryer took Keighley on a 10 per cent swing from Gary Waller, one of the Tory MPs who made headlines – 'Tory's love child lies' – during the 'back to basics' frenzy of early 1994. To add the final link to this chain, the mother of the 'love child' in question, Fay Stockwell, had been secretary to Sir Marcus Fox, the loser in Shipley. Politics can be a small world.

Beside Hornchurch on London's Essex borders lies Romford, rock-solid seat of the Tory knight, Sir Michael Neubert, and way down on Labour's target list at number 178. At least, with a 14,000 majority it had seemed rock solid. This time a 16 per cent swing saw him beaten, albeit by a margin of just 649 votes, and replaced by Labour's Eileen Gordon, a teacher. A remarkable 10,000 fewer people voted for Sir Michael than in 1992. In the Midlands, meanwhile, Sylvia Heal, who had won a 1990 by-election in mid-Staffordshire but lost the seat two years later, returned to parliament in style at Halesowen and Rowley Regis (target 3), turning a Tory majority of 125 into a Labour lead of 10,000.

And so it continued. Lab gain Pudsey (85). Lab gain Kingswood (36). Lab gain Vale of Glamorgan (1). The red strips were chasing each other across the bottom of the screen. Bedford (61), Coventry South (35), Cleethorpes (74) . . . They were landing faster than the Dimblebys could read them, let alone find meanings in them. Sittingbourne and Sheppey (150), Stourbridge (70), Leeds North West (91) . . . Faster than any viewer could take them in. Stockton South (66), Gloucester (58), Hove . . . Hold on. Hove? *Hove?* It was Paxman who spotted it; if the Conservatives can't hold that, he observed, something seismic must really be going on.

To most people, Hove is quintessentially Tory, the emblematic South Coast retirement home for colonels and civil servants who would never vote anything but Conservative this side of the Second Coming. Brighton's posher twin was not in Labour's top 90 target seats; it was not even in the top 120; it stood proudly at number 147 on the list, and few people would have expected to find it any higher. Yet now Hove had voted Labour. There was one person there who had never doubted that it would, and that was the winner himself.

Ivor Caplin, 38, a manager at Legal & General, always believed that events had conspired to make Hove a much better prospect than it looked. The demographics had changed, with the colonels moving out into the country; the sitting Tory, Sir Tim Sainsbury, had retired; and the council had gone Labour in 1995 with Caplin himself at the helm. 'We had an awful lot going for us and I always thought we were going to win,' he says. If he had been inclined to election-night nerves, he was spared them, for he was watching very closely when Peter Snow first showed off his graphics after the exit poll and he saw that one of the last blue seats to turn red on the predicted swing was Hove. His own count, it seems, was almost a formality: 'The trays of votes were piling up and it was clear all along we were 3,000–4,000 ahead.'

It was only when the result was announced – a majority of 4,000 and a swing of 16 per cent – that the emotion finally caught up with Caplin. The formal declaration in the small counting room was a subdued affair, but then the candidates made their way down to the packed public hall beneath. Just as Caplin walked in, the words 'Lab gain Hove' flashed up on the television screens there and the crowd went barmy. As he said later: 'Short of leading England out at Wembley, I can't imagine a better feeling than I had when I was walking out there. And in our own town hall, too.'

While others in the BBC studio struggled to find words for what was going on, Peter Snow had a twinkle in his eye. This was his moment; he had a trump card to play, and a relieved Dimbleby invited him to play it. 'Right,' he said. 'Now let's take a look at how Mr Blair's *targeting* of key seats is working.' With a swift punch of the air he was on his feet, legging it towards his screen.

The flap of his jacket pocket had gone askew and wires were sticking out of another pocket in his trousers, but he didn't care. 'We're going to have a look at the shooting gallery over here.' This proved to be a map of Britain with blue blocks all over it: Tory-held seats on Labour's target list. '*There* are the ones that have declared so far,' he said, and three-quarters of them disappeared, leaving about 25 blue blocks scattered over the map. Now we were ready; the camera swept to the side and we were approaching the island at speed from a point somewhere high above the Scillies.

It was like the Dambusters; no, it was like Luke Skywalker and the Death Star. Down we swooped over the West Country towards the nearest blue block and suddenly . . . Pow! it exploded, and up through the scattering blue debris surged a big red Labour block. 'There goes Kingswood!' cried Snow in triumph. Pow! It happened again. 'There goes Portsmouth North!' Pow! Pow! We were over London, bombing Putney and Battersea. Pow! 'There's Basildon, now a *huge* Labour majority.' Across the Midlands, Powpowpow! Red blocks everywhere. Into the north, Bradford, Leeds. Powpow! 'There's Stockton South!' Pow! And up to Scotland, pow! No wonder Snow looked pleased. This was his *pièce de résistance*, his Nintendo moment. If he had been carrying a revolver, he would have blown the smoke from the tip of the barrel, twirled it triumphantly and thrust it firmly into the holster at his hip. Beat that, Alastair.

Even as we were recovering, more big pows were in the making in Scotland. Dumfries fell to Labour. And then so did Eastwood, Glasgow's leafiest suburb and by some margin the safest Conservative seat north of the border. Eastwood had been held since 1979 by Allan Stewart, an uncompromising right-winger who had served as a Scottish Office Minister under both Thatcher and Major. He resigned from the government in 1995 after being accused of 'presenting' a pickaxe handle during a confrontation with some anti-road demonstrators; and then, just as the election campaign began, a tabloid reported on his friendship with a 'blonde mum-of-four' and he stepped aside as a candidate. A week later, Eastwood Tories were on the point of selecting the party chairman in Scotland, Sir Michael Hirst, to fight the seat, but he suddenly bowed out and resigned the chairmanship just before a second tabloid published another scandal story, this time about a gay relationship. In the end they found a candidate for the seat, but it was a hopeless case. Eastwood, Labour target 135, was captured on a swing of 14 per cent.

'Something very important is happening,' said Anthony King. 'The Conservative Party is becoming a minority English party. There's every chance that the Conservatives will have no seats at all in Wales after this election. It's perfectly possible that they will have at most one or two seats in Scotland. The Celts clearly don't like the Tories.' King went on to explain that over Britain as a whole Labour was not winning a particularly large share of the vote – no more than Harold Wilson had won when he squeaked home in 1964 – but that it was benefiting from tactical voting. 'Where Liberal Democrats don't think they have a chance they're going Labour; where Labour don't think they have a chance they're going Liberal Democrat. The Conservatives are simply being squeezed inexorably between these two forces.'

On ITV, Brunson was drawing attention to another big trend that was apparent now that 200 or so results were in. The 'red juggernaut', as he put it, was rolling almost unstoppably through the cities. In Birmingham and Manchester, Merseyside and Glasgow, Leeds and Sheffield, Coventry, Portsmouth and Norwich, the Conservatives appeared to be on the point of obliteration. A few seats were going to the Liberal Democrats, but overwhelmingly it was Labour that was gaining. In Greater London, which holds 74 seats, only a few had declared but almost every one was a Labour gain. Would the same happen there? Would the Conservatives become not just an English party but a country one as well?

It was time to intrude into private grief and ask the Tories the old, old question: how does it feel? 'Not available for comment' came the answer, and perhaps this was wise. John Suchet stood at Conservative Central Office with a grin on his face and explained that politicians were rarer there than hens' teeth. The crowd behind him were all journalists and 'we haven't set eyes on a Conservative MP here for something like two to two-and-a-half hours'. Cecil Parkinson, in the studio, applauded this low profile. 'We analyse the result in private; we don't squabble,' he said, but then he added: 'Quite frankly – and I'm being frivolous here – there don't seem to be enough people to have a good squabble.'

Like it or not, there was obviously a squabble in the making, and we caught a glimpse of it. Cutting across to Wokingham, Home Counties seat of the Tory arch-rebel John Redwood, we didn't actually hear him speak but we watched him, and very instructive it was. He stood on his own against a breeze-block wall and spoke intently into a mobile telephone. As he did so he was juggling a piece of paper (one of his own election leaflets) and a pen, and eventually he jotted down some notes. Somehow you knew this was a leadership bid in the making; it was like a scene from a modern-dress *Richard III*. Who was in? Who was out? How did it all add up? And according to the BBC's Anne Perkins, Redwood had been on the phone all evening.

What about Hezza? Would he be in the race to succeed Major? He wasn't talking either, but in his Henley constituency the BBC's Nick Witchell had received some valuable guidance from the next best thing, the 'friends and associates' of the Deputy

Prime Minister and First Secretary of State. Witchell reported: 'David, I think it is undeniable that the friends and associates of Michael Heseltine believe that if – I suppose one must start to think of when – John Major steps aside, that Michael Heseltine has the energy and the ambition, at the age of 64, once again to challenge for the leadership of the Conservative Party.' In what sounded from Witchell's description like an explicit job application, these friends and associates spoke of their man's 'stature and the experience' and insisted that he 'should not be wholly unacceptable' to the Euro-sceptics. 'They point out that it was Mr Heseltine who was responsible for the most controversial and perhaps the most effective Conservative poster of the election – the one with Mr Blair sitting on the knee of Chancellor Kohl.' Leadership material for sure.

CHAPTER FIVE

2 a.m. to 3 a.m.

*The rub of the green – Torbay by 12 – Harrogate regrets
– exit Lady Olga – a Galloway silence – Scotland
and Wales – carnage in Middle England – swinging London
– Kensington man – Euro-sceptic pain – the MP
for Harrods – enter the white suit – Tatton's verdict –
the Foreign Secretary – Mr Finchley – the cookie crumbles.*

In general elections, by and large, you win some and you lose some. Even if your party wins nationally, there are usually a few local disappointments to be swallowed – you drop a couple of seats that you thought were safe, or a promising frontbencher is defeated. By the same token, if you end up in opposition, you are still likely to score a few satisfying individual victories, safely defending seats your rivals have targeted, or bucking the trend with an upset or two. With 659 constituencies, there is ample room for the British people to express their diversity and occasional perversity – as when the voters of Bath spoiled the Conservative victory celebrations in 1992 by failing to re-elect the Tory Party Chairman, Chris Patten.

The 1997 trend had still not been bucked once. With a little help from the LibDems, Labour was cleaning up and the Conservatives had not so much as glimpsed a consolation prize. Their best result to date was the successful defence of Aldridge-Brownhills in the West Midlands, which had been number 128 on the Labour target list. Not much to boast about there. But the night was still young, and wise heads could reasonably expect a little cheer somewhere along the way. Perhaps a few of the Dicey Dozen might survive, and perhaps there would be a seat or two in Scotland. It wouldn't, it couldn't, be as bad as it looked. On the Labour and LibDem side the opposite feeling prevailed, underpinned by 18 years of habit; this is too good to be true, they were saying, sooner or later our luck is going to run out.

By the time Rupert Allason and the other candidates in Torbay mounted the platform to hear the result, after four recounts, there must have been many who had convinced themselves that this was going to be the first bit of luck to go the Tory way. ITV said the margin after the penultimate count was 22, while the BBC said it was just 2 votes, so it had all the makings of a traditional Liberal near-miss. To add to the poignancy, Adrian Sanders, the LibDem candidate, was already known throughout the party for his involvement in a previous disappointment: in the 1994 European elections he had narrowly failed to capture the Devon seat as a result of confusion caused by a 'Literal Democrat' candidate. In short, a certain LibDem fatalism appeared to be justified, and this was the more galling because a lot of people had been hoping to see Allason beaten.

A youthful 46 and himself the son of a Tory MP, Allason was famous as an author before he entered parliament in 1987. While still in his twenties he had gained the confidence of sources inside Britain's intelligence services, and the result was a series of revealing and commercially successful books on the history of MI5 and MI6, all written under the name 'Nigel West'. After he won the Torbay seat, Allason emerged from behind his pseudonym as a right-wing anti-European with a streak of arrogance that may have owed something to his private wealth. His most famous political act was to abstain in a crucial Maastricht vote without bothering to explain why, either in public or, apparently, in private. He simply went missing. When the furious Tory whips finally tracked him down, they kicked him out of the parliamentary party for a year. But at least Allason tried to keep on the right side of his voters, and the seat was not a real marginal. His majority was 6,000 and Torbay was 21st on the LibDem target list, needing a swing of 5 per cent.

Now, on an improbably colourful stage, he was waiting for the declaration. The backdrop was a vivid advertisement for Torbay, with a blue sky, a line of palm trees and a legend inviting us to the English Riviera. Centre stage stood a returning officer in town-crier robes, adorned with not one but two gold necklaces. 'It looks like a scene from *South Pacific*,' David Dimbleby remarked, 'you half expect them to burst into song.' Allason, however, was not singing; he looked very downcast among the palms, and we soon learned why. He had received 21,082 votes, while Sanders had 21,094. The Liberal Democrats had captured the seat by just 12 votes. 'No wonder there was a recount,' exclaimed Jonathan on ITV. 'If there's a majority smaller than that in this election, a lot of us will eat hats or whatever we've got.'

ITV had stayed to hear the outcome; the BBC pulled the plug on Torbay halfway through the declaration to switch to Harrogate and Knaresborough. That must have been frustrating for some, but for Harrogate it was a thrill, almost certainly the first time the constituency had ever declared on national television. After all, this had been a dull, safe Tory seat ever since Richard Dimbleby was a lad; now it was another LibDem target and, better than that, the Conservative candidate was Norman Lamont.

A little background. The outgoing Conservative MP for Harrogate, Robert Banks, had stepped aside, criticized for not being either seen much in the constituency or heard much in the Commons. There was a scramble for the vacancy and a strong feeling in favour of a local candidate, but when the smoke cleared Lamont had somehow won the nomination. Even by the standards of the former Chancellor of the Exchequer this was a remarkable career turn, for most observers thought he was finished in politics, another badly mauled casualty of the John Major years. Like David Mellor, Lamont had been a friend and supporter of Major in the late 1980s, and was rewarded with high office after Thatcher's fall. Black Wednesday severely dented his standing, however, and he did himself little good afterwards by suggesting that he had secretly wanted sterling out of the ERM all along. Reports that he had been singing *Je ne regrette rien* in the bath, which were presumably put about by his staff as proof of his sang-froid, only highlighted the ease with which this particular politician could slip into ridiculousness. The image of the stout, badger-faced Chancellor naked among the suds, doing gleeful Piaf impressions as he wielded the loofah, was not calculated to enhance his authority.

The Press was already exploiting this comic weakness. First, Lamont had been found to have a tenant who advertised herself as a 'sex therapist' and was happy to pose for photographers wearing only leather underwear and a broad smile. (Sniggers.) After he had evicted her it was alleged that part of the legal bill had been paid out of public funds. (Righteous indignation.) And part by a mysterious donor. (Indignant curiosity.) Then came Threshergate, a scandal about off-licence purchases. Did the Chancellor stop at a Threshers branch one evening and buy cheap champagne and a packet of 20 Raffles? Yes, said a shop assistant. To share with whom? asked a prurient Press, and a number of lurid insinuations floated by. Stop this nonsense, said Lamont, it's a pack of lies. Ultimately the Minister was proved right; it was untrue. But it was too late to save his dignity, especially since along the way we learned that the Chancellor of the Exchequer did not keep up his Access payments. (More sniggers, and many jokes about the Lamont Sector Borrowing Requirement.) Like poor Margot in *The Good Life*, it seemed this man was always the butt of the joke, and it was no surprise when in 1993 John Major heaved his old friend overboard. Thereafter Lamont embarked on a new career as an embittered Euro-sceptic who sniped from the back benches, supported Labour in key Maastricht votes and backed Redwood against Major in the 1995 leadership contest.

But Lamont had another problem. His old seat of Kingston in London was swept away by boundary changes and the successor constituencies did not want him. By some accounts he applied for 12 seats before reaching Harrogate; by others it was 13. Either way the view was widely held that he could not have landed this plum constituency without the help of Central Office or Number 10, and why they should have stepped in was the subject of some speculation. Perhaps it was out of pity, or perhaps to shut him up, to ensure, for example, that his memoirs were not published until *after* the election. Whatever the story, the Harrogate party set the condition that he must remain loyal to Major, and when it came to the election Lamont adopted a very low profile, which was perhaps the nearest to loyalty he could manage. This, however, placed him at a disadvantage in meeting the challenge of the LibDems. Their candidate, Phil Willis, a well-known local head teacher and the leader of the council, ran an intensive, aggressive campaign of the kind the party tends to mount in by-elections.

The mathematics of the seat were still on Lamont's side: with a notional Conservative majority of 9,000, Harrogate was way down at 56th on the LibDem target list and it would take a swing of 9 per cent before it changed hands. Squeezing Labour offered the LibDems little promise, since Labour wasn't strong enough to make much difference. By polling day the bookies were still tipping Lamont, but some LibDems were quietly placing big bets on their man. Willis himself, although he thought the campaign had gone well, did not bet: 'I half expected that 1992 phenomenon, when people went into the polling booth and their hands would quiver and shake and then be drawn, like on a ouija board, back towards the Tory candidate.'

When it came to the count, Willis chose to stay away as long as possible to avoid having to endure the tension in public. Instead, he sat in a friend's flat watching the early results and growing steadily more depressed at the sight of his party apparently being squeezed again. If Labour gained ground in Harrogate, Willis was done for. At midnight he had a call saying it was very tight. 'That was the very last thing I needed. It looked like we were going to be casualties of New Labour. I was really sweating. It was the worst hour of the whole campaign. And then, at about 1 a.m., my agent rang and used those famous words of David Steel's: "Mr Willis, prepare for government." We had a bundle of Lamont leaflets and we spread them out on the floor and my wife and I danced a ceremonial dance over them.'

At the count they found Lamont effectively in hiding, shielded from the Press and others by a phalanx of 'suits from London'. The two men shook hands before the declaration, at which point, Willis says, 'my wife felt sorry for him for the first time'. When the BBC cameras caught him, standing in line on the stage listening to the bad news, Lamont looked broken. He finished 6,000 votes behind Willis, and the Conservatives had lost Harrogate for the first time since 1906. One final humiliation remained. After Willis had said his words of thanks, the former Chancellor went to speak but was drowned out by a recording of *Je ne regrette rien*, played by some students in the hall who also unveiled a banner saying 'If it isn't hurting, it isn't working.

8. Norman Lamont hears his defeat announced in Harrogate.

Goodbye Norman'. His last, bitter words as he left were a threat to query the LibDem election expenses.

This result was followed by an exquisite moment of television confusion: what you might call a TV-warp. From the declaration at Harrogate the BBC producers cut directly to the crowd at the LibDem offices in London, who were watching on a big screen. They were plainly expected to cheer, but they showed no reaction at all, appearing hushed and tense. There was a simple reason for this: they were watching ITV, which was still showing the last seconds of the long declaration at Torbay. As we looked on they heard the figure for Adrian Sanders and realized that their man had narrowly beaten Allason to take the seat, and at that moment they erupted in joy. BBC viewers, under the impression that this was a delayed reaction to Harrogate, must have thought them rather slow-witted.

There had been a similar moment of cross-channel overlap earlier, when Jonathan Dimbleby interviewed Harriet Harman at her count in south London. While she was speaking a big cheer went up in the crowd watching television behind her and she was cruel enough to ask Jonathan on air what had happened. The crowd was watching BBC, so the poor man had no idea. He could only gulp helplessly for air while half his viewers switched channels to see what they were missing. As it happened, the result in question had been carried on ITV ten minutes earlier.

If we had stayed with that joyous LibDem crowd after Torbay and Harrogate, we might have seen them progress into a state of bliss previously unknown to liberal democracy, for in the two or three minutes that followed, the party also captured Aberdeenshire West and Kincardine in Scotland (one seat), and Carshalton and Wallington in London (ditto). 'LibDem gain' four times over: never have those words appeared with such frequency in so short a time, and Carshalton in particular represented a historic break-through into south-west London. At last, it seemed, their dominance of local government in the area was being translated into parliamentary seats. The winner was Thomas Brake, a local councillor, who defeated the veteran Tory Nigel Forman thanks to a 10,000-vote slump in the Conservative turnout.

There was more to come. In Hampshire, David Chidgey performed the extraordinary feat of holding on to Eastleigh. This was the seat left vacant in 1994 by the strange death of Stephen Milligan, and won by the LibDems on a 22 per cent swing. Chidgey was determined not to see it go the way of so many such gains – 'I wanted to be a proper MP and not just some by-election blip' – but statistics as well as precedent were heavily against him. Without the by-election tide and the resources that went with it, he struggled to canvass the whole constituency, and even on the doorsteps he did reach he couldn't trust the message. 'Our returns were absolutely brilliant,' he recalls, 'but I've fought a few elections now and the voters, bless 'em, they *always* say they'll vote for you. They're worse liars at elections than the politicians.'

Like Willis, Chidgey couldn't face spending time at the count, so he waited at a hotel near by, watching the results coming in on television. At 1 a.m. his agent called: he was about 1,000 votes ahead with two-thirds of the votes counted. He should come down now. No sooner had he arrived, however, than a recount was ordered and he had to sweat it out for another hour. 'I remember watching the television and seeing the other results come in.' The others were going wild, he recalls, 'but I didn't even react. I had just become dissociated from everything.' When the final figures were announced, however, he had scraped through with a majority of 754 votes.

Soon the LibDems had also won Twickenham, ousting another Tory old-timer, Toby Jessel, and Sutton and Cheam, where the victim was the extraordinary Lady Olga Maitland. This was another of those results which brought a smile to many faces in many parties and outside them, for Lady Olga is one of those professional controversialists who, over time, acquire a lot of enemies. The daughter of a Scottish aristocrat, she was working as a gossip columnist on the *Sunday Express* in the early 1980s when she won national attention as a woman campaigner *for* cruise missiles at Greenham Common. The Conservative Party warmed to her and in 1992 she landed this supposedly safe seat, allowing her to spend five years speaking up fearlessly from the Commons back benches in favour of such things as heterosexuality, Christianity and the family. Her high moment in parliamentary politics came in 1994, when she was formally rebuked and forced to apologize by the Speaker over a series of filibustering amendments which helped wreck the Civil Rights for Disabled Persons Bill. She had insisted the amendments were her own work when they were in fact written by parliamentary lawyers on government instructions. Now, with a 13 per cent swing, the voters of Sutton and Cheam had thrown her out. Leafy London was angry too.

In Scotland another Cabinet Minister was about to die by the sword. Ian Lang, the President of the Board of Trade, was probably best known nationally as the man who, in a formal Commons statement, attempted to portray the Scott report on arms sales to Iraq as a testament to the government's high-mindedness and honesty. Black, he tried to convince us, was white, and two plus two equalled three. Lang had first won his seat at Galloway and Upper Nithsdale in 1979 from the SNP, and now they were taking it back. On both sides this was a little piece of history – the senior Minister and former Scottish Secretary on the way out, the veteran nationalist Alasdair Morgan on the way in – and yet both men found themselves upstaged by an unlikely figure: the returning officer.

At first glance, James McGuire Smith looked the informal type: a smart cream jacket, blue shirt and lively blue tie, all beneath an attractively grizzled head and beard. None of your Torbay ceremonials here. No, Mr Smith wasn't formal at all; he was positively draconian. He had already written to every accredited representative of the Press, warning them that he would not hesitate to throw them out of his count if he wished. Now he was going to make his declaration and there would be no nonsense from anyone, Press or otherwise. 'I'm going to read the result for Galloway and Upper Nithsdale in one minute,' he announced in a thin, determined voice. 'Could I ask for total silence while I am speaking? Could I ask you to be courteous and polite to the candidates when they are speaking also? I will commence to read the result in 30 seconds.' In the pit before the stage was a crowd of not more than 60 people, a good few of them Press photographers. There did not seem to be too great a threat to public order, but you never know. Silence fell and Mr Smith began.

'I, James McGuire Smith, being the returning officer for the parliamentary election in Galloway and Upper Nithsdale, hereby give notice that the total number of votes polled for each candidate in the Galloway and Upper Nithsdale constituency was as follows: Katie Clark, the Scottish Labour Party candidate, six thousand, eight hundred and sixty-one. Six . . .' At this a number of people – three, or perhaps four – applauded. Mr Smith did not look up, but his expression was one of exasperation. He began again: 'Katie Clark, the Scottish Labour Party candidate, six thousand, eight hundred and sixty-one. Six, eight . . .' He stopped again. He had heard a noise. In the studio Jonathan Dimbleby muttered: 'He's making a bit of a meal of this.' Mr Smith's back straightened and his eyes combed the audience. 'Mr Flynn,' he said quietly. 'Could I ask you to assist those who have not been listening and do not wish to be courteous?' (Assist them? What *did* he mean?) And he began again: 'Katie Clark, the Scottish Labour Party candidate, six thousand, eight hundred and sixty-one. Six, eight, six, one . . .' Ms Clark had become famous beyond her entitlement, but the lesson was learnt: everybody behaved, and there was absolute silence. We got safely to Lang and his 12,825 votes, and then Morgan and his 18,449. But at this, alas, there was a big cheer and (horror!) a flag of St Andrew was brandished. Then a sudden, fearful hush. Mr Smith was not finished. Would he go all the way back to Katie Clark again? Or would it just be double detention all round? Silence. Tension. Mr Smith opened his mouth to speak. 'Alasdair Morgan, eighteen thousand . . .' Phew!

It was a show-stealing performance. 'They're very individual characters, these returning officers,' Jonathan said. Kirsty Wark on BBC Scotland observed tartly: 'I bet he's a teacher in another life.' In fact Mr Smith is a lawyer by training, and one of Scotland's more experienced returning officers to boot. It could have been worse. The Dumfries votes were counted in the same hall and during that declaration, made a little earlier, he had informed his audience: 'We can sit here all night if we have to.' If he had presided at Putney they'd be there yet.

So Lang was out. Aberdeenshire West had fallen to the Lib-Dems, and Edinburgh West soon followed. Perth and Tayside North were both lost to the SNP, and Dumfries, Stirling and Eastwood to Labour. Labour had also taken Aberdeen South, where the winner, Anne Begg, is a teacher who suffers from the crippling cell disorder, Gaucher disease, and she fought the campaign from her wheelchair. As the Tory dominoes fell, Peter Snow predicted that they would finish the night with just one seat in Scotland: Gordon. No sooner had he spoken than the LibDems won it, in a statistically remarkable fashion. This is a big rural seat, north of Aberdeen, held by the LibDem Treasury spokesman, Malcolm Bruce. He had won it by a whisker in 1992, but since then the boundary commissioners had heaped in so many Conservative voters that it was classified as a Tory seat with a majority of 8,500. Bruce needed a big swing merely to stay where he was, and he did it in style, with a huge 19 per cent shift from the Conservatives to give him a very comfortable 7,000 majority. This meant that Malcolm Rifkind's Edinburgh Pentlands seat was the last Tory toehold north of the border; in principle there was little chance of him withstanding the swing, but perhaps even at this late hour Scotland's Conservatives might have their moment of luck. The Edinburgh tellers were still at work.

Wales was looking even bleaker for the Conservatives, if that was possible. Cardiff North (target 40) went the way of so many other leafy urban seats, to Labour. The Vale of Glamorgan had already gone and Clwyd West (101) and Monmouth (41) followed. A complete Tory wipeout was now a racing certainty and Snow stepped forward with another little history lesson to put this in context, displaying the same graphic with towers which he had used to illustrate the long Conservative decline in Scotland. Unfortunately, although the label in the corner said 'Wales', the screen showed the same figures as before – the Scottish figures, with 36 seats in 1955 and so on. Snow looked a little disconcerted, but skipped lightly over this gremlin without confessing. The truth is that the Tories have never done well in Wales and their peak in this century was the 14 seats won in 1983. That slipped to eight in 1987 and six in 1992; now it was about to be zero. David Dimbleby, sharing with Snow a dogged enthusiasm for nineteenth-century analogies and precedents, pointed out that it was 100 years since the Conservatives had been so unpopular on the Celtic fringe. Then it had been the Liberals who dominated Scotland and Wales, but as Anthony King pointed out rather tetchily, there were not too many useful parallels here: Gladstone, he said, had been dead a long time.

The carnage in Conservative England, while not so complete, was still too much to take in. Like a great scythe sweeping across the country, the Labour vote was cropping seats even Peter Mandelson had never dreamed of. To the west, Shrewsbury (target number 115) had fallen, as had Wansdyke (119) and Swindon South (105). On the south coast, Brighton Pavilion (34) had joined Hove as a Labour seat. Outside London there were St Albans (126) and Luton South (9) – Luton South being the place where John Major had mounted his soapbox on 17 March to set the long election campaign rolling; the voters responded by giving Labour a majority of 11,000. Heading northwards, there was Tony Marlow's seat at Northampton North (47), now Labour, and Amber Valley (17). Broxtowe (94) and Gedling (108), both outside Nottingham, had returned Labour MPs, as had High Peak (53). To the east Waveney (48) and to the west Anthony Eden's old seat at Warwick (106) had fallen to Labour, as had both seats in Bury (54 and 11). Further north, Wyre Forest (96), Elmet (38), Batley and Spen (15), Middlesbrough South (18) and Tynemouth (42) all became Labour seats.

As Brunson had anticipated, the urban map was transformed. Glasgow was entirely red, and Cardiff, and all of Newcastle and Sunderland, Leeds and Bradford. Of the 15 south Yorkshire seats – Barnsley, Doncaster, Rotherham and Sheffield – all were red bar one: the LibDems' Hallam. Merseyside was heading the same way. Greater Manchester comprised 28 seats and of those only two remained blue: the distant southern suburbs of Altrincham and Cheadle. In the West Midlands, Birmingham, Coventry, Walsall, West Bromwich, Wolverhampton and Dudley were all Labour.

What about London? While the LibDems had marched into the south-western suburbs, Labour too was advancing in force, and from several directions at once. In the east they had captured Upminster (144), Hornchurch (109) and Romford (178), and they now added both Ilfords (30 and 164). In the west they won Hayes and Harlington (2), Ealing North (89) and Brent North (160). This last had been the seat of Margaret Thatcher's old acolyte, Sir Rhodes Boyson, whom we saw sitting, hunched and disappointed, trying to come to terms with the evaporation of his 10,000 majority. To the south, Labour won Croydon North (5) and Croydon Central (143). Mitcham and Morden (22), which borders Carshalton and Sutton, now fell to Labour and Dame Angela Rumbold, whose supporters had earlier been so optimistic, was not just defeated but trounced. A 16 per cent swing saw this former Deputy Chairman of the Tory Party beaten by a margin of 14,000 votes, and at the declaration she looked desperate to escape. In neighbouring Wimbledon (177), of all places, another 16 per cent swing saw Labour's Roger Casale replace the Conservative Charles Goodson-Wickes.

These swings were proving even bigger than in the rest of the country. 'If tonight is quite as historic as we all believe it is,' Alastair Stewart said, 'then London is at the heart of the story.' He stepped aside to make way for some virtual reality, and up from the floor in front of him leapt the pillars of a bar chart. They were just a foot away from him, and you wanted him to reach out and try to touch. But he didn't. Labour, the pillars showed, was winning 50 per cent of the vote in the capital, against the Conservatives' 35 per cent, while the swing to Labour in the capital was over 13 per cent, against a national average of under 10. At this rate the Tories would be lucky to keep a dozen seats out of the 74 in the capital, down from the 41 seats they had won in 1992.

North London had still not spoken, but there was every indication that it would be just as good for Labour. And, sensationally, there was a growing feeling that Michael Portillo, the Secretary of State for Defence, was in real trouble in his seat of Enfield Southgate – number 190 on Labour's target list. The BBC's Lance Price had already reported from there that the piles of votes, as they stacked up, were surprisingly close. Now he warned us that 'it looks, from all the indications we are hearing from all the parties, that Michael Portillo has lost his seat here'. ITV's reporter took the same view, but warned that we would have to wait a while for the final confirmation. Brunson shook his head in disbelief. 'I don't know where this evening's going to end, do you?' he asked. 'It's extraordinary.'

One little glimmer showed for the Conservatives in the metropolis, although the party leadership might have been in two minds about it. Right in the heart of London one of the safest Tory seats in the country did its duty and returned the Conservative candidate without ado. The notional majority of 22,000 was cut to a real one of 10,000, but at least the seat of Kensington and Chelsea was still safe. Whether the new MP was safe was another matter, however, for he was Alan Clark, self-confessed philanderer, incurable scandal-monger and the man who blew open the arms-to-Iraq affair. Or, to put it another way: Alan Clark, the historian, millionaire and former Trade and Defence Minister.

Clark captured the nomination in Kensington and Chelsea with his usual *élan*, following the reluctant departure from politics of Nick Scott. A popular wet, Sir Nicholas in recent years had become as accident-prone as Lamont or Mellor. In parliament he was Olga Maitland's accomplice in the government's shameful wrecking of the bill to extend civil rights for the disabled, while in private life he became embroiled in controversy after walking away from a minor road accident involving his car and a push-chair containing a Swiss toddler. ('What's the big deal?' his companion was reported to have said. 'The child's not dead and they're not even English.') It surprised few that it all became too much for Scott, and eventually for his constituency association. It surprised many that Clark applied for the nomination, and that he got it. Clark had retired as MP for Plymouth Sutton in 1992 and then had made a fortune (to add to his several other fortunes) from his diaries. The fear was that, in this most sociable and convenient of seats, he was proposing to spend his time gathering or creating scandalous material for the sequels.

If the return of Alan Clark offered little satisfaction in the desperate Tory search for silver linings, then the fate of the Euro-sceptics may have consoled at least some. At his Huntingdon home even John Major (still, like most of the country, watching events unfold on television) might have managed a small, thin smile at the defeats of Nicholas Budgen, Tony Marlow, Toby Jessel, Rupert Allason and Norman Lamont, all rebels who had caused him trouble over the years. And perhaps there was a secret chuckle at the prospect that Michael Portillo, one of the Cabinet 'bastards' of whom he had complained to Brunson, might go the same way. Not, it should be said, that there was any evidence that the voters were singling out Tory opponents of Europe for punishment; it was just that they were making no distinction. As both Brunson and Oakley remarked, it didn't help in the least to be a Euro-sceptic. Major might have found consolation in that.

There was every sign, however, that the European argument in the Conservative Party was far from over. From Billericay, where she was awaiting her result, a flirtatious Teresa Gorman appeared on ITV. Our man spoke as if trying to catch her eye: 'It's Jonathan Dimbleby here, trying to have a word with you.'

'Oh really,' she replied, swinging towards us, 'that's sweet of you.'

'I know it is. I'm a very sweet fellow.'

When they got down to business, Teresa, among the most dogged of Euro-rebels, insisted she had been right all along. 'I'm afraid it's just one of those occasions when our policies have not been what the Conservative voters in the country wanted. On the doorstep in my constituency, time and time again, people said that they were going to support me because of my views on Europe.' At Conservative Central Office someone whom Jon Sopel described as 'the architect of the campaign' but who chose to remain nameless, had voiced similar opinions off-screen. The party, he said, had made a mistake in not choosing the 'nuclear option' of a categorical rejection of the single currency. This was nuclear because it would probably have meant the resignation of the Chancellor, Ken Clarke.

Clarke himself, safely returned in Rushcliffe despite the mayhem around him in Nottinghamshire, tried to stay aloof. Now, he suggested, was not a time for blood-letting; enough had been spilt already. With one eye clearly trained on the leadership, he made light of his Tory critics and seemed to blame the media. 'My own view is that I would have liked to have seen more about the economy in this election,' he said. 'I'd have liked to have heard a lot less about Europe and obviously I'd like to have heard a lot less about sleaze. But no party can completely control the agenda. The modern media, the modern election, has a life of its own.'

Sleaze, as he suggested, was proving to be a millstone round the neck of the Conservative Party. Matrix Churchill, the Pergau

Dam affair, Homes for Votes, Jobs for the Boys, Back to Basics, Lord Archer's share deals, Cash for Questions – the years since John Major stepped into Margaret Thatcher's shoes had been replete with stories that gave the electorate cause to wonder about the probity of their politicians, and particularly their Tory politicians. When it came to the election, it looked as though the voters had decided to lump sleaze together with everything else and punish the party as a whole, rather than singling out those who were directly involved in scandal. Tim Yeo, for example, whose affair and illegitimate child had cost him his position as an Environment Minister during the 'back to basics' days, was returned to parliament without fuss by the voters of Suffolk South. There was a swing against him of 11 per cent, but on this night that was nothing special.

One constituency, however, stood out as exceptional: in Tatton, the leafy Cheshire seat of Neil Hamilton, the issue was sleaze and nothing else. This was not because of the gravity of the charges against Hamilton – by the standards of the Major years the sums and misdeeds involved were hardly extravagant – it was a matter of timing, character and accident. Tatton had become a test of public anger about sleaze, a sort of controlled experiment in which all variables and complicating factors were stripped away so that we could determine beyond doubt whether people really cared about it, and what they were prepared to do. The verdict of the Tatton voters was now due.

The Neil Hamilton sleaze story had begun, like so much else, in the 'greed is good' days of the late 1980s. Mohammed al-Fayed had beaten Tiny Rowland in the battle for the ownership of Harrods, but Rowland would not give up. He waged a campaign, often through the pages of his newspaper, the *Observer*, to show that al-Fayed had come by the store dishonestly, by lying about his wealth. Al-Fayed fought back. These were extremely wealthy men, and they fought dirty.

Hamilton was elected to parliament in 1983, on the crest of the Falklands wave, and he was one of a group of right-wing backbenchers who amused themselves and pleased their betters by taunting and interrupting Neil Kinnock every time he spoke in the Commons. Hamilton was also vociferous on privatization and the iniquities of trades unions, and he attached himself to the party's backbench committee on trade and industry. In this capacity, in 1985, he became useful to al-Fayed. The link was made through an old friend of Hamilton's, the parliamentary lobbyist Ian Greer.

Hamilton and a number of other Conservative backbenchers now took part in a concerted lobbying effort to prevent a Department of Trade and Industry inquiry into the al-Fayed fortune and the Harrods takeover for which Rowland was pressing. When the inquiry was ordered, they tried to discredit its proceedings. When it was completed, they asked for the report to be suppressed. When a leaked version was published (by the *Observer*) they rubbished its contents. Those contents, incidentally, were damning for the reputation of al-Fayed, the inspectors concluding that he had lied repeatedly in his business career, but there was no suggestion that Harrods should be taken from him. Hamilton, in letters to and meetings with Ministers, and in questions and motions in parliament, doggedly tried to shield al-Fayed and turn the attack on Rowland.

Skip forward a few years to the early 1990s. Miraculously, al-Fayed and Rowland have kissed and made up, but the Harrods boss is now angry with the Conservative government, partly because the DTI report has been allowed to stand as a stain on his good name and partly because he has encountered unforeseen difficulties in acquiring a British passport. Since he has done much to boost the British economy, and since he has contributed £250,000 to Conservative Party coffers, he regards this as unfair. He decides to get even, so in 1994 he takes his story to the *Guardian*. He tells the newspaper about the MPs who acted on his behalf, and he claims that he paid some of them for what they did. These payments were not declared by the MPs in the Commons Register of Interests. He says, moreover, that Hamilton (who by now has become the junior minister responsible for business probity) personally received from his own hand brown envelopes containing thousands of pounds in £50 notes. Hamilton had also received payments in kind, notably a free week's stay with his wife at the Paris Ritz Hotel, another al-Fayed property.

When these sensational allegations were published, another junior minister who was implicated, Tim Smith, confessed and resigned. Hamilton, however, denied the story and issued a writ for libel against the *Guardian*; but he was still forced from office. Noisily and persistently over the following two years he protested his innocence and attacked the newspaper. Then, on the very eve of the libel trial in September 1996, he and his co-plaintiff, Greer, suddenly and sensationally agreed to drop the case and pay £15,000 towards the *Guardian*'s costs. They pleaded that they did not have the funds to fight a rich newspaper. The *Guardian* responded with a front-page assault on Hamilton beneath the headline 'A liar and a cheat'.

There was one more twist to the story before the election. The papers of the case were passed to the Parliamentary Commissioner for Standards, Sir Gordon Downey, for his verdict on whether the rules of the Commons had been broken. Sir Gordon's report on this and other cases of 'cash for questions' was complete or very nearly complete when, on 17 March 1997, John Major called the election. Once parliament was dissolved, however, the report could not be published. This was presented, by the *Guardian* among others, as the last cover-up of the Major government; the electorate would vote without knowing the truth.

In the heat of controversy, Tatton Conservative Association gave Hamilton its endorsement, accepting his word that he was the victim of malicious fabrications. Although they would have dearly loved to see this embarrassing man swept aside, Conservative Central Office and Downing Street were powerless to displace him. Thus it was that Hamilton became a symbol in the general election, either as the candidate for sleaze or as an innocent man pilloried by the left-wing Press.

While the scandal unfolded, the boundary commissioners had done Hamilton a huge favour by lopping an industrial corner off his constituency and giving him highly exclusive (and Conservative) Alderley Edge instead. His majority, which had been a sturdy 16,000 in 1992, was now calculated at 22,500; Labour and the Liberal Democrats combined would not have come within shouting distance. So, for all the clouds hanging over him, Hamilton seemed assured of re-election, and his critics, by the same token, appeared powerless to call him to account.

For a week attempts were made to secure a recall of parliament, which would allow publication of the Downey report, and it was when those efforts failed that Labour had a bright idea. What if they and the LibDems withdrew their candidates in Tatton in favour of a single, non-party, anti-sleaze candidate? It might well persuade the Tatton Tories to dump Hamilton when it came to formal adoption in a few days' time, and if it didn't, then the Mr Clean candidate, whoever he was, could go all the way. The idea caught on; the LibDems agreed and, after a brief search for the appropriate personality, Martin Bell was recruited.

Bell is BBC Television's old warhorse, one of that breed of itinerant foreign correspondents who can tell you how many wars they have covered (in his case it is 11). His long and courageous work in the latest of those wars, Bosnia, had finally elevated him at the age of 58 to the status of a news star, in the way that such reporters as Kate Adie, John Simpson and Mark Tully had been stars before him. As with Tully, Bell's trademark is the short, blunt sentence, delivered without inflection. 'It was another bad day in sniper's alley. Four people wounded, including a woman and her baby son. The Serbs said they weren't doing the shooting. Nobody down here in Sarajevo believed them.' In a very difficult and complex situation British viewers came to trust his judgement, and their trust was reinforced when he described, with knitted brow, the dilemmas he faced. Could he remain impartial when confronted by atrocities? Could he remain calm when confronted by Western indifference and incompetence? Anxious, conscientious and somehow always in the right place, our Martin could cope.

Approached, at the Labour Party's initiative, through a chain of friends, he agreed to stand. Labour and the LibDems duly stepped aside and he blundered, innocent and unbriefed, into the Tatton election. Suddenly this corner of Cheshire had, as one reporter put it, slipped into a parallel political universe. Neil Hamilton had one rival who would fight him on one issue and who was not inclined or able to play by the normal rules. 'Your vote can beat Hamilton', said Bell's literature, above the words: 'Trust. Honesty. Integrity.'

Hamilton's strategy was to paint Bell as a creature of Labour headquarters and of the *Guardian* who was just another assailant in the unfair vendetta against him. This he did with sufficient success to persuade his constituency association formally to adopt him, by 182 votes to 35, with 65 abstentions. So it was a fight to the finish, man to man. Or not quite, because at this stage the British public became aware of something that Westminster had known for years: Hamilton was a double-act, and his wife Christine was something to be reckoned with. Blonde and slightly horsy, she was outraged by what was going on and was quite happy to say so for the cameras. Bell, she declared, had 'a flaming cheek' coming to Tatton, since he had 'nothing at all to do with Cheshire' but was instead a representative of the corrupt London media, living in Hampstead. Many found her abrasive but, compared with her husband, who grew oilier and shiftier by the day, she was positively refreshing.

Bell was not merely taking on Neil and Christine; he was taking on history, for the age of the independent MP was long past. No candidate free of party affiliation had been elected to the Commons for a British seat since 1945; the last of them was the author and wit, A. P. Herbert, who represented Oxford University – the university seats disappeared in 1950. All

9. *Martin Bell (right) met Neil Hamilton and his beaded wife Christine in Tatton.*

experience since then proved that the British political system and the British voter did not like free spirits or single-issue crusaders. And it wasn't at all clear whether Bell was *for* anything; he was just against sleaze and Hamilton and what he called with deliberate quaintness 'conduct unbecoming'. Besides refusing bribes, no one had any idea what he would do in parliament if he was elected.

Would the voters buy it? A week before voting an opinion poll suggested that Bell had 50 per cent support in Tatton and Hamilton 38 per cent, but as with every other poll in the election nobody was ready to believe it. One Bell activist remarked that voting for Hamilton was like sinning: nobody admitted to it but most people probably did it. By the close of voting on Thursday Bell himself thought he might win by 2,000 votes, but he did not believe that this was a convincing enough rebuff for Hamilton.

At 2.42 a.m. the candidates in Tatton's parallel political universe took their places in readiness for the declaration. First on was Bell himself, wearing his usual cream suit and accompanied by his daughter Melissa, whom he described as his spin doctor. He moved to the extreme left of the stage. After him came a clutch of fringe candidates, eight in all, of whom one deserves special mention. Burnel Penhaul, alias the Transformer, was a tall Birmingham drag queen running on the Miss Moneypenny Glamorous One ticket. He wore a birdcage in his hair throughout the campaign and courted voters with the slogan: 'I'll put the tat back into Tatton'. Entering now from stage right, he appeared as an eight-foot scarlet PVC peacock, complete with glittering fantail, tutu and a monumental head-dress that appeared to be made of brown bananas. So high were his platform shoes he could scarcely walk, but with great determination he tottered to a point directly behind the podium where, towering over all the others, he made a perfect centrepiece to the Tory blue backdrop.

Hamilton, accompanied by Christine (her motto is WDTT – We Do Things Together), was one of the last on stage, taking up position on the extreme right.

Briskly the returning officer got down to business, and the first total he announced was Bell's: 29,354 votes. There was a cheer, and Bell bit his lip and did some bashful fidgeting. Then came a minor candidate with a hundred or so, and then came Hamilton: 18,277 votes. The most extraordinary electoral contest in British politics in decades had ended with victory for Bell by the generous margin of 11,000 votes. In ultra-Conservative Tatton, in Knutsford, Wilmslow and Alderley Edge, the man with convictions but no politics had captured three out of every five votes cast and comprehensively routed the sitting Tory MP. This was plainly a parallel universe in which the laws of gravity did not apply.

'Ladies and gentlemen,' Bell said, taking the hand-held microphone, 'I believe this is a proud moment for the people of Tatton, though I have to say a rather humbling one for me. I did not do this. You did it. It was not my victory. It was your victory, though maybe there was a time – when I received the endorsement of Sir Alec Guinness – that I knew the force was with us. I believe you have lit a beacon which will shed light in some dark corners and illuminate the mother of parliaments itself. It is a strong signal to the rest of the country, which will be heeded.'

Heartfelt words, but at this moment even the most enthralled of viewers could not fail to notice, just behind the head of the man in white, the straining bodice of the drag queen in red. Nor the beefy hands on the hips, which wiggled occasionally to catch the eye. Nor, above all, the strange, curving, breast-like appendages, also in red PVC, which appeared to hang on either side of Bell's grey locks. This was putting the tat into Tatton all right. Thank goodness Bell couldn't see what we could. He went on, nobly and seriously: 'I shall be and shall remain independent. I shall take no party whip. I shall serve for one term only. I am deeply grateful to all of you, and may I just repeat for the last time a couple of lines from G. K. Chesterton that I used during the campaign. "Smile at us, pay us, pass us, but do not quite forget / We are the people of England, and we have not spoken yet." You have spoken tonight, magnificently, and I thank you from the bottom of my heart.'

Hamilton, the more practised candidate, pointedly made up for Bell's failure to thank the police and everybody else involved in running the election. Clutching the microphone shakily in both hands, he went on: 'I have been proud to represent the Tatton constituency for the past 14 years and of course am devastated at the result here this evening. I know it will come as a great disappointment to all those who have worked so hard to attempt to elect me for the fourth time.' He aimed a couple of jibes at Bell and quoted from Churchill, and then concluded with the promise that he would be back 'as a politician and as a man' once the Downey report had cleared his name. 'This is *not* the end of the road,' he declared. 'This is *not* the end of my political career.'

John Major probably didn't see the Tatton declaration, since he was at that moment making his way from his home in Great Stukeley to the count at Huntingdon. Arriving there, he emerged with Norma, looking characteristically calm and serious. While the Tory world fell around his ears, he knew that at least here he was safe, and that the voters who had elected him since 1979 would not reject him. But whether he actually wanted another five years at Westminster was another matter. At the age of 54, by any standards he had an extraordinary career behind him – after six years and five months in Downing Street, this uncharismatic man had outlasted such figures as Attlee, Lloyd George and Heath – and politics could have nothing more to offer him. Some of his ministerial colleagues were already speaking of him in the past tense, and those who talked of him staying on temporarily were doing so only for their own ends. The question for Major was not whether he would resign but when.

Tony Blair, meanwhile, was making his way from Trimdon Labour Club, where he made an emotional speech of tribute to the people of the local party, to Teesside airport. There he stepped from his car, shook a great many hands with enthusiasm, gave a double thumbs-up signal and, with his eternal companions Cherie and Alastair, mounted the steps into the private jet which would take him to London. With half the results in and the forecasts suggesting Labour would finish with a majority of 177, he was on his way to the party.

Across the country the seats were continuing to fall. Leeds North East was target 57 on Labour's list and thus was the constituency they needed to win for an overall majority. Much fuss had been made of it before the election, with reporters visiting the scene to ask whether Labour could manage it. It was now gathered in without difficulty and without fanfare, easy meat on a swing of 12 per cent. Derby North (target 49) and Gillingham (167), Warrington South (31) and Calder Valley (52), they rolled in one after another. Here and there Conservatives held on, but nothing disrupted the pattern of Tory defeats in the cities, or in Scotland and Wales.

Had Martin Bell still inhabited *this* political universe, he would have spent the night in Edinburgh and not Cheshire, for he had been booked by the BBC to cover the count which would decide the fate of the Foreign Secretary, Malcolm Rifkind. Given Rifkind's line on British policy in Bosnia – he resisted and delayed increases in British involvement, even as Bell argued with passion on television that to stand aside was akin to a war crime – this may well have been a piece of mischief. But Bell now had other fish to fry, so he was denied the chance of seeing the Foreign Secretary suffer.

Rifkind had been MP for Edinburgh Pentlands since 1974 and, after some anxiety, he survived the 1992 election with a decent majority of 4,000. In many ways he is the caricature of the posh Scot, pinstriped and with a plum in his mouth to distort what was already a strange accent. His grin, his domed forehead and his heavy glasses add to the comic effect, but his record speaks of something serious. This was another former Secretary of State for Scotland, as well as a former Transport and Defence Secretary. At the age of 50, Rifkind still had hopes of capturing the Tory leadership and, to that end, in recent years he had slid sideways into mild Euro-scepticism. But if he was to rise further he needed a seat and, with all else gone in Scotland, he now looked as forlorn as the boy on the burning deck. As they mounted the stage the smile was still there, and the olde-worlde courtesy, but there was no reprieve for him. Rifkind polled 15,000 votes and Labour's Linda Clark polled 20,000; the swing was 10 per cent. Another one bit the dust.

For Scotland this Tory oblivion was historic. Three Scottish Secretaries, three Cabinet Ministers, three stout opponents of devolution, all beaten in a single night, and no one left north of the border to step into their shoes. There had been nothing like this before in all the years of parliamentary democracy. Who would speak for the Conservatives on Scotland, or *in* Scotland? It would have to be some Scot representing an English seat or, worse still, an Englishman – Englishmen had already served in the Welsh Office. And if the Tories had seemed to many Scots a foreign, even a colonial party when Rifkind, Lang and Forsyth were in charge, what hope was there for them now? As for the devolution question, they were left isolated and discredited, comprehensively rejected by the voters. As more than one commentator pointed out, it seemed that their best hope was to cast aside their objections and embrace the idea with enthusiasm, in the hope that the subsequent elections in Scotland and Wales would enable them to acquire some sort of representative presence there.

North London now spoke, at last, with four big gains for Labour. Hendon (121) fell to them, and Edmonton (10), and Enfield North (104) and, believe it or not, Finchley and Golders Green. Finchley was the seat Margaret Thatcher had held from 1959 to 1992, the middle-class, upwardly mobile constituency which, in the words of her biographer, Hugo Young, was 'demographically and physically congruent with her personality and her politics'. David Dimbleby captured this congruence perfectly with a slip of the tongue on an earlier election night, when he referred to Thatcher as 'Mrs Finchley'. Oddly, however, the figures never quite did justice to the match, for Labour always put up a good fight in the constituency and Mrs Finchley had to content herself with majorities in four figures. Her successor in the seat, Hartley Booth, squandered the inheritance somewhat, becoming the victim of a classic tabloid kiss-and-tell exposé when his young researcher revealed their affair and his love poems. (Her name was Emily Barr and, to the satisfaction of Tory conspiracy theorists, she went on to become a *Guardian* journalist.)

Despite this, the Labour threat to the seat had, in the view of most, been removed by radical boundary changes which tied Finchley to Golders Green and doubled the Tory majority to a notional 12,000. This pushed it right down to number 142 on the Labour target list. No wonder Rudi Vis, the Dutch-born academic who was the Labour candidate, was expecting to lose.

No wonder he had made no preparations for departure from his post at the University of East London, or from Barnet council, where his was one of two votes keeping Labour in power. But it happened. The swing was 15 per cent, and he landed a majority of 3,000. 'It's going to be very difficult to sort things out,' Vis said wistfully.

Things were looking very bad indeed for Michael Portillo. Finchley, Enfield North and Edmonton were all neighbours of his Enfield Southgate constituency, and the swings in any of them would be enough to see him out. The BBC, in fact, was reporting categorically that he had lost by 1,700 votes, and certainly the camera shots of the Defence Secretary in the final stages of his count did not show the face of a winner. Where, as Brunson had asked, would it all end?

Anthony King pointed out that it was very rare in British elections for Cabinet Ministers to be defeated and this time three had already gone, even before Portillo's result. 'It looks as though there is going to be one of the biggest culls of Ministers this century. The Conservatives in 1945 lost five members of the Cabinet – including, it must be said, Harold Macmillan, who went on to do good things.' And it wasn't just the Cabinet, he explained. 'It looks as though, of all the Ministers who are defending Tory seats tonight, two-thirds are likely to lose their seats. A lot have already gone. We've had Ian Lang, Michael Forsyth, Tom Sackville, Alastair Burt, John Bowis, Sir Nicholas Bonsor . . . They're going down like ninepins.' At which a *distrait* David Dimbleby remarked: 'OK, thank you. Well, that's the way it crumbles. Jeremy?'

CHAPTER SIX

3 a.m. to 4 a.m.

Vaulting ambition – a hopeless cause – Portillo
defeated – red Midlands – Waldegrave – overall majority –
swingometers dumped – Aitken's fate – victory at
Hastings – champagne socialism – the party
party – Exeter chooses – Major safe – Dorrell's sources –
Hanley – Worcester woman.

Michael Portillo had tasted election defeat before, and not just in some no-hope Labour stronghold. In the general election of 1983, when he was a young party insider and speech-writer, he was selected to fight the marginal seat of Birmingham Perry Barr, and he blew it. He not only failed to win the seat but, against the national trend, saw Labour increase its majority dramatically. After such an unpromising debut, a year later Portillo was fortunate to be adopted as candidate for a by-election in Enfield Southgate, a leafy slice of London suburbia. Again he had problems pleasing the voters and, although this time he won the seat, the Tory majority slumped from 16,000 to 5,000. Memories of the disappointments and anxieties of those distant days may have gone through his mind as he sat out the last moments of his count – having second thoughts, perhaps, about Paxman's offer of hemlock.

Despite that shaky start in 1984, Enfield Southgate proved a good friend to this paradoxical man, the son of a left-wing Spanish intellectual who turned into a fervent free-marketeer and shameless flag-waver. He soon rebuilt the majority, and in

1992 it was 15,500 – big enough, in the words of one election handbook, to make it 'a secure base from which Portillo's ambition may vault'. And ambition he had aplenty.

Within two years of being elected he had his foot on the escalator of promotion, serving as a whip and later as a high-profile junior minister at Transport and Environment, before entering the Cabinet in 1992, at the age of 39, as Chief Secretary to the Treasury. Along the way he established his right-wing credentials, becoming a leader among the generation of 1983 Conservatives – they included Peter Lilley, Michael Forsyth and a close personal friend, Neil Hamilton – who were most iconoclastic and single-minded in their Thatcherism. On a personal level he was charming and thoughtful, and had the gift of inspiring loyalty. And his party conference speeches, full of bombast, defiance and what passes in that forum for jokes, won him an enthusiastic following in the wider Conservative Party. This was a rising star.

In that part of the country which did not vote Conservative, however, Portillo was acutely *un*popular. On ideological grounds he had closely espoused as a Minister two sensationally unpopular policies: railway privatization and the poll tax. (Of the latter, he said, memorably: 'It will be a vote winner.') And he was frequently on television, first defending the Thatcher government in its twilight and then speaking up for the Tory Right in the new, divided dawn ushered in by John Major. There was something about this man, with his combative style, his blithe certainty, his quiff and his thick, short neck squeezed into a high, white collar, that got up people's noses. So it was with a mixture of glee and revulsion that much of the country looked on in 1994 as the Enfield Southgate Tories threw a lavish party for their man at Alexandra Palace to mark his ten years in parliament. It looked like the purest hubris (and Portillo himself was said to have been deeply embarrassed).

From about 1995, by which time Major had promoted him to Defence Secretary, Portillo was the right-wing front-runner for the party leadership. He had rivals, such as Redwood, Howard and Lilley, but his base was broader than theirs and his appeal in the party stronger. The 92 Group and the No Turning Back Group, the main right-wing clubs of Tory MPs, both backed him, as did Margaret Thatcher herself. Yet when in the summer of 1995 Major threw down the gauntlet to his 'bastard' critics by inviting leadership challengers, Portillo made a mess of things. He didn't stand, but he didn't get any points for loyalty either, since his supporters were caught in the act of preparing a campaign headquarters for him. It was the wacky John Redwood who led for the Right and, although he failed, his status was enhanced. Portillo blew it again at the party conference that autumn with a much-mocked speech – Brussels was bad and the SAS was good, he said, in terms so crude they would have shamed a school debating society. In the constituency, too, he slipped up, endorsing the unpopular sale of the party headquarters there to McDonalds, and the subsequent loan of the proceeds to Central Office. And yet he was doing no worse than his rivals, so that on the eve of the election he was still deemed to be the man most likely to succeed.

Stephen Twigg was a schoolboy in Enfield when Portillo was first elected as his MP, and the two actually met when Portillo spoke at his school. Eleven years later, in February 1996, Twigg was selected by a majority of one vote as the Labour challenger for the seat. He was still only 29 but, like the young Portillo, he had started early in politics and had some useful experience under his belt – chair of the National Union of Students, local councillor in Islington, researcher for Margaret Hodge and then secretary of the Fabian Society. He did not, however, expect to win a parliamentary seat at this first attempt. 'I thought it was a challenge to go home and be the Labour candidate there, and maybe put a dent in Michael Portillo's majority.'

These were the 1992 figures in Enfield Southgate: Conservative, 28,390; Labour, 12,845; LibDem, 7,072. And there had been no boundary changes since then to improve the picture. A 16 per cent swing was required for a Labour victory, and the constituency was way, way down at number 190 on the party's target list. It looked beyond hope – all the more so since its low ranking meant that, instead of being a seat into which Labour poured effort, local activists were actually diverted out of the constituency to work in more winnable seats near by. 'We were a very small operation; some days only four or five people would turn up to do the work. We targeted the marginal parts of the constituency, leaving the Labour areas and the real Tory areas alone,' Twigg recalls. Although the doorstep returns were promising, he discounted them. 'I remembered a story I had been told of a Tory who stood in a safe Labour seat and was convinced it was going really well, until she was really trounced. I kept telling myself not to trust impressions.'

It wasn't until four days before polling that his absolute confidence in his own defeat was shaken. The *Observer* published a poll of selected constituencies which suggested that the gap in Enfield Southgate was as narrow as four points. If LibDems voted tactically in Twigg's favour, the *Observer* said, then Portillo would be out. 'Up to then I had thought to myself that it would be good to get his majority down below 10,000,' says Twigg. 'But even after it I didn't think I would win. I just thought we might get him down to 5,000. Suddenly, however, we were getting dozens of people turning up to help.'

By election day, Gallup put Portillo just two points ahead within the margin of error, but a local bookie (aware, no doubt, that in the normal run of things nine out of every ten predicted election upsets do not happen) still tipped the Defence Secretary to scrape home. On the night, after the polling stations closed, Twigg went to a French restaurant with some party workers, and of the eight people present only one predicted a Labour win. That one person was not the candidate. 'I did *not* go along to the count thinking I was about to be elected a Member of Parliament,' he says – Enfield was no exception to the national state of denial. When the boxes were emptied out, the old party sages were divided about the auguries, but the majority view was that young Twigg would not make it. Then the bundles began to pile up. Twigg recalls: 'A woman spectator started shouting to me, "You're 800 ahead." "You're 1,100 ahead." I went a bit nearer and I saw she was right. From about three-quarters of the way through I was consistently ahead.'

Portillo did his early stint on BBC ('It is likely,' Paxman had told him, 'that you will be one of the few Cabinet Ministers who keeps his seat') and went to his constituency HQ around 11.30 p.m., appearing immediately on ITV and giving no intimation of his plight. By then, however, reporters were sniffing something sensational in the Enfield air. The BBC's Lance Price gave us a warning but still hedged his bets: it could be very tight, he said. At 1.30 a.m. word of the danger had reached the reporters at Tory Central Office, but Price was still reporting that Labour didn't quite believe it could win. It was a little after 2 a.m. that Price promised us 'perhaps the most extraordinary result' in a night of extraordinary results. At almost the same moment ITV said that it 'looked very much as though' the Minister would lose his seat.

There was about half an hour to go when Portillo reached the count, and he looked stern and thoughtful. He knew. Seeing Twigg, he greeted him with the words: 'You must be shattered.' Twigg smiled and said he was. The two men had met three times since that 1985 encounter at Twigg's school: twice during the campaign and once a few months earlier, when Portillo, in an unusual gesture, invited his LibDem and Labour challengers to lunch at the Commons. Now they stood together for a few moments, talking about the national picture, Portillo express ing surprise at the scale of the Tory defeat. Then the returning officer called the agents and candidates together and they huddled as he read through the figures, the usual procedure. 'Everyone happy?' he asked when he finished. 'Ecstatic,' said Portillo.

Votes from three constituencies were being counted at Picketts Lock Leisure Centre, and the results were ready all at once. Enfield Southgate, as luck would have it, was last in the queue to declare, so the candidates had to stand around waiting for half an hour. Twigg was, as Portillo had suggested, stunned. He had never expected to win, and indeed it had been a condition of his appointment at the Fabian Society that he would not enter parliament. But they would forgive him. For Portillo, who much of the time was watched by cameras, these must have been very long and uncomfortable minutes. For 13 years, ever since he had scraped into parliament, his career had followed a relentless upward course on the ladders of power, and until that night he must have worried much more about Ken Clarke as a rival than Stephen Twigg. Now he was slipping down a very big snake. Whatever plan he and his many powerful friends had made for the contest to succeed John Major, it was all worthless.

At last they were called on to the stage and the returning officer got ready to read the figures. As they took their places something strange happened. Suddenly it was Portillo who looked relaxed, his fingers lightly interwoven before him and a slight smile on his lips. Twigg, a tall, dark figure at the end of the line with all three buttons of his jacket done up, assumed the same stance as his opponent, but he did not look comfortable. He shifted uneasily and wore a grim expression. It was he who was behaving like a loser. The results came: the LibDem got 5,000 votes, the Referendum Party 1,350 and a fringe figure 200. Twigg, his hands now joined behind his back, was rocking back and forth on his heels, still looking anxious; Portillo was serene. And then: 'Portillo, Michael Denzil Xavier . . .' At this there was a ripple of laughter and the returning officer called for silence. He resumed: '. . . Conservative Party: nineteen thousand, one hundred and thirty-seven.' Silence. Then came another fringe candidate with 300 votes, and finally: 'Twigg, Stephen, Labour Party: twenty thousand . . .' The rest was lost in wild cheering.

Twigg's face at the moment of triumph was transformed. First there was a broad, boyish smile, then an intake of breath which lifted his shoulders as if he was shrugging off a great weight, and finally he raised and rolled his eyes extravagantly in disbelief. 'It

10. Stephen Twigg applauds Michael Portillo in Enfield.

was an expression I couldn't repeat, a mixture of elation and bewilderment, a combination of emotions that remained with me for about two weeks,' he said later. But it was something else as well, like a schoolboy guitarist who finds himself on stage jamming with a world-famous band. 'Gosh, look at me,' it said.

The BBC cut to another face: a shocked Gillian Shephard in Norfolk. And then to a tactfully expressionless John Redwood in Wokingham, and finally to a seething, dancing, cheering, raving Labour throng at the Festival Hall in central London. Mellor's defeat had raised a big cheer among the growing crowd of revellers there, and Lamont's a bigger one, but this trumped everything. As ITV's Julia Somerville put it, if there were such a thing as a scream-ometer in the hall, then the news of Portillo's defeat would have sent it 'into the red and beyond'. David Dimbleby, as ever, was more sober. 'Labour celebrates,' he said, 'as the Thatcher favourite, one of the bastards in the Cabinet as John Major called him, is defeated by young Stephen Twigg.'

Labour won in Enfield Southgate by 1,500 votes after a swing of 17 per cent. Compared with 1992, Portillo's vote was down by 9,000 and the LibDem vote down by 2,000. Of those 11,000 lost votes, 2,500 might be accounted for by a drop in turnout and a further 1,350 by the Referendum Party. The rest presumably went to Labour, up by 7,000. Thousands of people, in short, switched straight from Tory to Labour, while many LibDems clearly voted tactically to get Portillo out. And the Tories couldn't even blame Sir James Goldsmith, for even if all the Referendum Party votes had gone to the Conservatives, Labour would still have won by 91 votes.

Twigg hadn't prepared a victory speech. 'Once or twice in the bath I had amused myself by imagining what I would say if I won, which was just as well because bits of that came back to me.' He shook hands with the losers and then stepped forward.

'This result,' he said, 'along with other results all over the country, demonstrates that there is no longer such a thing as a no-go area for the Labour Party.' He thanked the usual people – police, other candidates, returning officer, party activists – and then paid special thanks to the 20,000 people who had voted for him. 'Those who voted Labour consistently through the difficult years as well as the good years for Labour; their loyalty and consistency has been repaid with this result. Thousands of first-time voters. Thousands of people switching from other parties, especially the Conservatives, and hundreds of Liberal Democrats, who put aside their national preference and voted tactically for Labour to ensure a non-Conservative victory. I pay tribute to all of them, and I will serve as the Member of Parliament for all of them, and indeed for the people who didn't vote for me. It's been a good night for Labour and a good night for me, but you've all been here a long time and you probably don't want to hear much more from me. We've got a long night to celebrate and the weekend as well. Thanks a lot.'

Portillo had been smiling since the result, and he applauded Twigg. Now he spoke: 'My first duty is to congratulate Stephen Twigg on his victory . . . I think he'll be a very good Member of Parliament and I wish him well with it. We're obviously also going to have a new government. The government has to represent this country and do its best, and I wish the new government well.' He thanked local party workers, and then he turned to the national scene: 'A truly terrible night for the Conservatives. I would have wished to be part of rebuilding it inside the House of Commons; I can't now do that. But I would like to do whatever I can from the wings to help rebuild a great party which has a great future. One thing alone I will not miss, and that's all the questions about the leadership. Thank you very much.' Another smile, and he turned on his heel and returned to his place.

'Nothing befits the man so well as the manner of his passing,' concluded Ian Duncan Smith in the BBC studio. The Tory MP for Norman Tebbit's old seat of Chingford, Duncan Smith was confident of a resurrection: 'I know he'll be back; it's just a matter of when.' Gillian Shephard took the same view: 'He will be enormously missed,' she said, 'but of course he will be back.' For all the brave words, though, there was no doubt that Portillo's absence transformed the landscape of their party in a manner which pleased Labour as much as it displeased them. Not only were they suffering a humiliating defeat, but now the very man whom the survivors would probably have chosen to rebuild their fortunes had been swept away. For Labour it was almost too good to be true; was *this* the end of the winning streak?

No. Across the bottom of the screen it was still 'Lab gain', 'Lab gain', 'Lab gain'. Many of these seats were on the original list of 90 constituencies where Labour had concentrated its fire, like Tamworth, which had been target number 69 and was now won with a majority of 7,500. Redditch, target 44, was safely gathered in, and Burton (46), where Sir Ivan Lawrence, the Conservative Chairman of the Home Affairs Select Committee, was ousted. 'I spent an afternoon canvassing with Ivan Lawrence to see how it was,' Michael Brunson recalled, 'and like so many of the Tory candidates this has come as a *total* bolt from the blue for him. Ivan was saying quite honestly, "It seems all right to me. I know what the polls are saying, but I'm not having doors slammed in my face."' In the privacy of the polling booth, the voters of Burton went one better than slamming the door. A 9 per cent swing gave Labour a 6,000 majority there, the first time it had won the seat since 1945.

Also in the Midlands, Labour captured Erewash (target 59), Milton Keynes South West (63), Leicestershire North West (14) and Newark (84). More surprisingly, they took Wellingborough (113), albeit by just 187 votes, and Northampton South (156), by 744 votes. A great splash of red was spreading south, connecting Labour's old Nottinghamshire stronghold and the West Midlands, and another big splash was appearing further south around Northamptonshire. In Wales the mopping up continued, with victories in Conwy (71), and Preseli (12), although Plaid Cymru held on to Ceredigion, which had been target 92. To the north there were victories in Chorley (28) and Bolton West (55). In Yorkshire, Colne Valley (76) became a Labour seat, and further east Brigg and Goole (83) on the Humber and, on a 15 per cent swing, Scarborough and Whitby (117). Norfolk North West (107) fell to Labour, which meant that the royal palace at Sandringham now had a Labour MP. And a swing of 14 per cent took Great Yarmouth (68) from that Tory Euro-rebel who always looked like a misprint, Michael Carttiss. By now both Norwich seats as well as Great Yarmouth and Lowestoft (in the constituency of Waveney) were in Labour hands. Urban East Anglia had really swung.

To the south, Brighton Kemptown (122) became a Labour seat, giving the party the full set of three – Pavilion, Hove and Kemptown – in the queen of resorts. In the south-west, Alan Clark's old seat of Plymouth Sutton (16) switched to Labour, making Plymouth another city without Tory representation, and outside Gloucester, already captured, the eternally Tory constituency of Stroud (97) returned a Labour MP. Bristol, too, was going the way of the other big cities and, just ten minutes after Portillo's defeat, it produced another Cabinet casualty in William Waldegrave.

Waldegrave is an old-fashioned Tory wet who, in the view of many, sold his soul to the Right for the sake of promotion and always, in consequence, looked worried. In youth he was an academic whiz-kid in Edward Heath's think-tank and then was a critic of Margaret Thatcher's brutal early economics, and for this he was rewarded with nine years in a succession of junior ministerial posts. Only when she had gone did a subdued Waldegrave make it into Cabinet, as Health Secretary. This was followed by an inglorious spell as Minister responsible for the Citizen's Charter (and the traffic cones hotline); then he was Agriculture Secretary and finally he became Chief Secretary to the Treasury, the cake-cutting job. This last was a back-room post and may have suited him best, for that worried look and his tendency to get into scrapes meant that he was never at ease in a high-profile department.

In 1996 he paid one last, reluctant visit to the furnace of public hostility. In the 1980s he had been one of the junior ministers most closely involved in the dubious decisions which led to the arms-to-Iraq scandal, and he was the only one of them still in high office when the Scott Report was published. Had he lied about the rules on arms sales? Scott, characteristically if mysteriously precise, cleared him of 'duplicitous intention' but linked him, with others, to the lesser misdemeanours of 'misleading' and being 'designedly uninformative'. He survived.

Now he stood before us in Bristol at the age of 51, beaten by Labour's Valerie Davey, a teacher and county councillor six years his senior. It was a remarkable result, and not only because the Minister, MP for Bristol West for 18 years, should have been safe with a notional majority of 9,500. In 1992 Labour had finished third, some way behind the LibDems in second place. Now Davey had leapfrogged into first place. Waldegrave was visibly saddened, and said with just a hint of bitterness that Labour had better do well in government since they were inheriting 'the strongest economy in Europe'. All of Bristol was now in Labour hands, and neighbouring Wansdyke and Kingswood, while the LibDems held Bath and Northavon. In this part of the country the blue rinse was being thoroughly washed out.

Labour needed a minimum of 330 seats to hold a majority in the House of Commons and, as that point approached, the ITV team paused for breath. Jonathan Dimbleby, more than anyone else on the night, had usefully kept reminding us how far removed all this was from the usual experience of election night. He pointed out that, so great was the swing, there was no such thing as a safe Tory seat any more and that what were once thought to be highly significant marginals were being nodded through as routine Labour gains. Now, as the scoreboard clicked up the 328th seat for Labour, he said we would wait and watch until we reached the historic milestone. 'Alastair,' he said, to fill the moment, 'what do you make of this?'

Stewart replied: 'One of the staggering things about that number is – and Stephen Twigg in Enfield Southgate is a very good example – there are a huge number of young men and women who are entering that new House of Commons for the Labour Party who thought they were out for a trial run.'

The number went to 329. Stewart went on to point out that on the opposition benches there would be only three Tories for every Liberal Democrat – 'staggering' – and the LibDems would really be a force to be reckoned with. Michael Brunson said he was struck by how young the Commons would be, not like the stuffy place he was familiar with, while Jonathan remarked again on all the towns and cities which no longer had Tory MPs. It was an amiable interlude, like countless other conversations taking place in homes around the country: three men simply sharing their astonishment.

Then it came: the 330th Labour seat. 'Here we have it,' said

Jonathan, putting on his historic voice. 'We now officially declare that Labour, the Labour Party, has won the 1997 general election!' At this an electronic message, perhaps even a virtual one, passed round the studio at balcony height announcing: 'Election result: Labour victory'. A cheer went up, which Jonathan first tried to pass off as coming from Sue Lawley's panel of voters, but then he admitted it had come in part at least from the ITV election night staff. Over on BBC, the milestone was passed with less ceremony, as we cut away abruptly from Peter Snow in mid-flow to a neon sign at Piccadilly Circus which read: 'BBC '97 Election Update: Labour Victory'.

These television teams were still struggling to cope. Just like everybody else, they were not prepared for anything on this scale. As Jonathan Dimbleby admitted: 'In rehearsal beforehand we were on 0 per cent, 3 per cent, 4 per cent . . .' Here there were swings of four times that, and more. The swingometers, designed for less exotic circumstances, had been dispensed with, while the battleground graphics were also unable to do justice to a rout. Alastair Stewart's battleground arrangement, in big type with columns of constituency names beneath each percentage figure, was fine up to 5 or 6 per cent, but then he had to shuffle the whole lot to the left to see what was happening in the 9 and 10 per cent zone, and he had to do it again to see those really big swings such as Enfield Southgate and Crosby. The effect of overview was lost. Peter Snow's battleground was more compact, but that made it appear crowded and cramped; the truth was that this transformation was so big it was proving very difficult to illustrate.

And the results were bunched. From 2 a.m. on, they came in so rapidly that sensational upsets, such as the Labour victory at Wellingborough and the defeat of Olga Maitland at Sutton and Cheam, were passing across the screen unremarked. David Butler pointed out that this was the first general election since the war in which more than 100 seats had changed hands, and the final figure would certainly be very much higher. There simply wasn't time to discuss them all, or even to show the full figures for every gain and loss. And so rapidly did one big upset succeed another – Tatton, Pentlands, Finchley, Enfield, Bristol – that there was hardly a moment in between to crunch the numbers and review the trends. The Dimblebys, anchoring all this, responded in contrasting ways: David was calm, slick and professional, always comfortable company; Jonathan was enthusiastic and wide-eyed, less fluent perhaps, but often more engaging.

The result that pushed Labour into power may well have come from Thanet South, on the corner of Kent; it was certainly in the crush at that moment. This particular event vividly illustrated the difficulties of the television producers, for it was another headline-maker, and yet they didn't have either the cameras or the time to show it, or even to have it discussed. It was the defeat of Jonathan Aitken.

Like both William Waldegrave and David Mellor, Aitken had been a Treasury Chief Secretary under John Major; like Rupert Allason, he was an author and had a Tory MP for a father; like Alan Clark, he was wealthy and moved in the most exclusive circles; like Michael Portillo, he was charming and thoughtful in private but sometimes graceless in public; and, like Neil Hamilton, he had stayed in the Paris Ritz. Aitken certainly belonged in the company of 1990s Conservative politicians, and yet he was no mere composite but a true original.

He sprang from a lesser branch of the Beaverbrook tree and inherited some money, but nothing too lavish. He went to Eton and Oxford and from there slipped effortlessly into the Tory political and social world. He proved to be a little wild and unpredictable, however, and soon offended the Establishment by passing to the *Sunday Telegraph* some secret official papers about arms sales to Nigeria. He had expected to be offered a safe Tory seat, but doors suddenly began closing to him, so he set off to earn some money. These were the Heath years and he did well, launching Aitken Hume International and working for Slater Walker. It was in this period that he made the acquaintance of members of the Saudi royal family, and in time he became an agent for their investments.

In 1974 he was elected MP for Thanet East and soon afterwards began what might have been a politically useful romance, with Carol Thatcher. But it was not to be, and legend has it that mother Margaret never forgave him for making Carol cry. Whether even she was capable of picking and rejecting government ministers on such grounds alone seems doubtful, but the fact remains that Aitken spent the entire Thatcher era on the back benches. In that long interlude his wealth grew, his Middle Eastern connections flourished and he acquired something else: an air of mystery. How did he get so rich, with a plum house on Lord North Street, a mansion in his constituency and fingers in so many pies? Stories were told and doubts were raised; a cloud, of suspicion or envy, hung over him. But John Major wasn't worried, and he made up for Thatcher's neglect as soon as she was out of the way, giving Aitken the job of number two at the defence ministry. This was a brave appointment for a man with close links to the Middle East and to the arms trade, but Aitken was soon regarded as a success.

In October 1994, when Mohammed al-Fayed decided to lash out at a Tory government he had come to hate, he not only gave the *Guardian* the Neil Hamilton story, he also gave it the dirt on a more important figure, Jonathan Aitken, by then Chief Secretary and a member of the Cabinet. A year earlier Aitken had stayed at the Paris Ritz (prop.: M. al-Fayed) and run up a large bill. That bill, the *Guardian* now alleged, was paid by Said Ayas, personal assistant to a Saudi prince. This was surely a strange and improper way for a British government minister to behave. Aitken denied the story, insisting that the bill had been paid by his wife.

Five months later, another scandal broke, this time concerning his role as a non-executive director of a British arms firm, BMARC, which was accused of breaking an arms embargo on Iran in the late 1980s. He denied any knowledge of the covert sales. And then in April 1995 came the last straw, when *World in Action* produced the allegation that the Minister had tried to procure girls for visiting Arab businessmen. Aitken resigned from the government and, in a moment of high theatre, announced that he was going to 'cut out the cancer of bent and twisted journalism' using 'the simple sword of truth and the trusty shield of British fair play'. In other words he was going to sue.

By the time the election came around, however, the case had not come to court. On the face of it re-election seemed to be a formality. He had been an MP for 23 years and his majority last time out was 11,500. His constituency, now called Thanet South, was number 140 on Labour's list, requiring a swing of nearly 12 per cent.

Local Labour activists, however, always thought they could defeat him. They had five years of solid progress in the constituency behind them: in 1992 they overtook the Liberals to claim second place; in 1993 they made big gains in county council elections; in the 1994 Euro-elections they edged ahead of the Conservatives in the popular vote; in 1995 they captured Thanet council. None of this, it should be said, impressed the Labour leadership at Millbank, which rejected all suggestions that the seat was winnable; like Enfield Southgate, Thanet South was supposed to help other Labour constituencies and forget its own fight. This it chose not to do.

Stephen Ladyman, 44, a computer expert and councillor who had stood for Labour in Wantage in 1987, was selected to take on Aitken, and he waged a vigorous campaign, leaning heavily on the new council's experience and record. Aitken's spell as MP was characterized as 23 years of decline for Thanet (which by some measures has the second-highest unemployment in the country). Aitken's well-known anti-European stance was also turned against him: it was Brussels and not London, Ladyman argued, which threw a financial lifeline to the constituency. As the election progressed, Conservative Central Office became sufficiently concerned to send in reinforcements.

For two years Ladyman had been as certain of victory as Stephen Twigg was of defeat, but on the night of polling day he wavered. His canvassing hadn't been quite as thorough as he would have liked, and he was worried by the Tories' late push. He thought there were about 1,000 votes in it either way. As counting began he watched the rows of bundles build up and could see he was running neck and neck with Aitken. Then a third row appeared between the two main ones, and more votes were added there. None of the party observers could make out whose votes they were, but they were obviously now crucial to the result. 'Everybody was trying to see, and they were ignoring everything else they should have been doing,' Ladyman recalls. 'Eventually a man came over and picked up the bundle, and everybody ran across to see what he was going to do with them. He slapped it down and I saw it was mine.'

Ladyman had won, on a 15 per cent swing, by a margin of 3,000 votes. Jonathan Aitken, having waited patiently for 16 years to become a minister and having then resigned after five years in office under a cloud of scandal, was now, two years later, out of politics altogether. He was stunned. 'Despite all you hear,' says Ladyman, 'he is a difficult man not to like when you meet him; not at all arrogant. During the campaign he was never less than a gentleman and we had good debates, with, I think, respect on either side. I felt rather sad when I saw him looking so miserable.' Sleaze seems to have played little part in Aitken's defeat, for the voters showed little interest in the specific allegations against him. The swing against him, moreover, was probably not personal, since it was matched by the swing in Thanet North (where the sitting Tory had started with a bigger majority and so managed to hang on).

Elsewhere in the south-east Labour was rampant. In Kent, Dover (13) was recaptured after an interval of 27 years, and Hastings and Rye became a Labour seat for the first time ever. The competition to be the most improbable of all Labour gains was tough, with Wimbledon, Crosby and Hove in hot contention, but this was surely the winner. Held for the Conservatives by Jacqui Lait, the first Tory woman whip, Hastings was a constituency where Labour had captured just 16 per cent of the vote in 1992, finishing a poor third. To the LibDems it was target 33 and their candidate, Monroe Palmer, was fighting it for the second time. To Labour, nationally at least, it wasn't a target at all, since it languished down at number 225 on the list. And yet, as with Thanet South and Hove, there were some hidden grounds for optimism.

Hastings is not quite the comfortable place it once was: tourism and fishing have declined and it has become a place where local authorities dump their homeless. A lot of people in Hastings, moreover, are elderly without being well-off, and they were hit by Norman Lamont's decision to impose VAT on heating fuel. They would not lightly forgive him his singing in the bath. The Tories no longer had a single seat on Hastings council, which was split almost evenly between the LibDems and Labour, and Labour was fielding as candidate Michael Foster, a well-known local solicitor, who had fought the seat three times in the 1970s.

Foster wasn't even aware that the constituency came so low on the party's target list, which was based on the 1992 election figures when the Conservatives had received 25,500 votes, the LibDems 19,000 and Labour 8,500. 'I wouldn't have stood if I hadn't thought we could win,' he says. He knew from his 1970s experience – when he got within 4,000 votes of the Tories – that Labour could do much better. The canvassing went well and, like Stephen Twigg, Foster received a boost from the *Observer* the weekend before voting, when it reported that he was leading a three-way fight. 'We got copies of that through every door we could. It gave people the confidence that it was actually worth voting Labour.' Now he won the seat, and comfortably. Labour got 17,000 votes, the Conservatives 14,500 and the LibDems 13,500. The swing was 18.5 per cent.

The seats along the Thames Estuary, once a Tory heartland, were now Labour's too. After Gillingham, Basildon and Sittingbourne and Sheppey, all captured earlier, came Dartford (target 86) and Medway (102), and then Gravesham (64), the constituency which always changes hands when the government changes. Most unexpectedly, Labour also won Castle Point in Essex, once described as 'the utopia of the property-owning democracy', which had been target 189. In London, already the scene of 17 Labour gains, there were four more: Brentford and Isleworth (19), Harrow East (112), Harrow West (196) and Bexleyheath and Crayford (137). Harrow East had been the seat of Hugh Dykes, the most ardent of Conservative Euro-enthusiasts; now for once he had something in common with sceptics such as Nicholas Budgen and Tony Marlow.

The new towns and satellite towns, too, were tumbling. To

the south Crawley (23) fell, and for the first time ever Labour had an MP in West Sussex. On the other side of the capital, Luton North (81) joined Luton South in the Labour fold, as did Hemel Hempstead (99), Watford (82) and Harlow (21), the seat of that flamboyant Tory, Jerry Hayes. And in another new town, Stevenage (37), Barbara Follett duly won a place in parliament at her third attempt. This victory was the occasion for a memorable celebration, captured lovingly and almost in its entirety by the BBC.

By way of a photo-opportunity, the Folletts in their moment of glory had ready a jeroboam of champagne which they proposed to crack open for the cameras and, perhaps, splash around, racing-driver style, in a show of exuberance. When the camera found them they were posed and ready, Ken to the left, neatly coifed and suited, holding the big bottle, Barbara in the centre, beaming in red, and to the left a very large young man in a red shirt bedecked with badges. To hand was a table full of flute glasses. 'In Stevenage the Folletts appear to be about to celebrate their victory there,' said David Dimbleby, surveying this little scene with a jaundiced eye. Barbara duly gave the nod to the big fellow, who gripped the cork, draped in a cloth, and began to twist. 'A Grand Prix-sized bottle of champagne,' David continued with satisfaction, 'which won't open.' And sure enough it was putting up a fight.

Ken held on tight as the young man tugged away, making desperate faces, but there was no pop, no fizz. 'I think the thing to do is shake it,' said David helpfully, 'and the cork will pop out.' They couldn't hear him, but they had the same idea; nothing happened. The big fellow tried twisting instead of pulling, but nothing happened. While everybody in the crowd around them gave advice, Ken's smile became strained and Barbara lent a hand. Nothing. 'There's going to be the most terrible explosion

11. *Ken and Barbara Follett with bottle at Stevenage, ready for the Great Struggle.*

in a moment,' said David, brightening up considerably. The young man tried wiggling the cork back and forth. Still nothing. 'The agony of celebrating victory in Stevenage,' said David. Then we heard Ken observe: 'This is the most interesting photo-opportunity of the entire election campaign.' He may well have been right; not since Neil Kinnock fell in the sea at Brighton had a Labour stunt provided such unintended amusement.

We had been watching this performance for one minute and ten seconds, an eternity in television news time, when David could take no more. 'I think it's time to listen to a chorus of "Things Can Only Get Better" from the Festival Hall,' he said, 'and leave them to their fate in Stevenage. They'd obviously be better off with orange juice.' And we left them. We glimpsed D:Ream in action before the massed ranks of Labour youth, playing what Dimbleby called 'the song which drove everybody mad on the campaign bus', but barely a verse had passed before we were back with Ken and Barbie and the big bottle. It looked like something was about to happen, for a large and purposeful moustachioed man in a suit had his hands on the cork, while Ken and the lad in the red shirt held the bottle. There seemed to be hands everywhere and a huge effort in train, but the cork still wouldn't budge. We cut back to D:Ream, and then quickly back to Stevenage to see yet another pair of hands, this time a woman's, enter from stage left. No joy. 'We'll keep you abreast of Stevenage as the night goes on,' David promised. And then, while the Great Struggle proceeded on the huge tellywall behind him, he produced the line we had all been aching for: 'They were called champagne socialists, but they are clearly very incompetent champagne socialists.'

After two and a half minutes, with Dimbleby on the point of giving up altogether, there was a sudden movement over his shoulder. The man with the moustache stopped struggling, lifted the cloth from the top of the bottle – and produced the top half of the cork. Abject failure. The rest of the cork was still stubbornly doing its business, keeping drinkers from their bubbly and viewers from their overdue image of Labour jubilation. Ken Follett tried to laugh some more but looked fed up, and Dimbleby decided enough was enough. 'That's it! Right!' he said, thumping the E-table. 'Francine Stock at the Royal Festival Hall! I hope the Labour Party *there* is being rather more successful.' By the time we got back to Stevenage to witness champagne being poured, fully five minutes had passed since our first visit. In the end they had resorted to a corkscrew.

ITV missed the Stevenage affair, but it was at the party at the Festival Hall. 'A scene of very great delight,' said Jonathan Dimbleby.

Brunson explained: 'They promised their workers and their supporters this party, win or lose. Obviously it would have been slightly different had they lost . . . Now they have their night of celebration.'

Yes, Jonathan chimed in, 'And even their opponents would say that they deserve that celebration.' Politics was a rough business, he said, but 'when you win you allow yourself a frisson of pleasure'.

It wasn't long before we returned there for another frisson, courtesy of Julia Somerville, who told us the joint was really jumping. 'I said it was bedlam before; I don't know what the next step up from bedlam is,' she said. 'Don't you think it's sometimes a characteristic of people who are incredibly buttoned up that when they do let go they *really* let go?' This party had been planned secretly for some time, as Brunson suggested, but news of it leaked out to the papers a few days ahead and caused the Millbank eggheads some anxiety (shades of 1992 and premature Labour triumphalism at the Sheffield rally). That's when the 'win or lose' line came out, although the idea of a party at such a venue on the night of another Labour defeat doesn't bear much thinking about. Throughout election day, Labour officials and Festival Hall staff had toiled to prepare the venue, and the first guests (such as Richard Branson) began to arrive after 11 p.m. But even here the champagne socialists had some problems, for in the wait to reach the 330-seat mark the bottles warmed up and began to pop of their own accord. In the end all was well and just before 3.10 a.m. the toast was drunk.

So, too, Julia implied, were a few of the guests. 'The champagne is flowing,' she said. 'My producer's very excited because he has just been embraced by a semi-naked woman.'

'Have *you* managed to preserve your integrity?' Jonathan inquired.

'Have I managed to have a drink?' Julia replied, pushing her earpiece harder into her ear.

Jonathan, clearly wishing he was at the party himself, pressed on: 'Have you looked after yourself all right there?'

'I'm doing very well, thank you,' came the reply. With that we were treated to a full minute of D:Ream and the infamous theme tune, to the improbable accompaniment of messages at the bottom of the screen announcing 'Lab hold Bolsover' and 'Lab hold Ellesmere Port and Neston'.

There were still plenty of victories to be won, and plenty of results to test the scream-ometer. The battle for Exeter, Labour's target number 32, had been an especially bitter one, so the outcome was awaited with great interest.

The Labour candidate was Ben Bradshaw. Bradshaw was a tall, young, good-looking, award-winning BBC foreign correspondent, which might seem a good start, but he had taken on this seat relatively late, and in inauspicious circumstances. He was selected in September 1996, after the Labour NEC had ordered the de-selection of John Lloyd, a barrister. Lloyd had been expecting to stand for the second time and, having increased the party's vote in Exeter by an exceptional 50 per cent in 1992, he was looking forward with some confidence to winning. Then came an extraordinary series of events.

Originally a South African, in the early 1960s Lloyd had taken part in minor acts of terrorism against the apartheid regime, helping to blow up electricity pylons and the like. He and most of his accomplices were arrested and, after some psychological torture and a long spell in solitary confinement, Lloyd effectively turned state's witness. Accounts vary as to the weight and importance of his evidence, but one of his associates, at whose trial he testified, was subsequently executed. Lloyd left South Africa soon afterwards. He had told his constituency party and people in local government in Exeter of his past, and it had caused no problems. But in 1995, as the likelihood increased that he would become an MP, South African exiles in Britain brought pressure to bear on Labour to have him barred as a candidate on the grounds that he had betrayed the struggle against apartheid and had never apologized or atoned. The case was explored at length in the national press and the Labour leadership grew uneasy. The local party stood by Lloyd – more than that, they fought tooth and nail for him – but in the end he was disqualified.

Bradshaw was not a local boy, but he had spent his training period with the BBC in Exeter and was known there, which helped him win the selection. Another factor may have been a certain local bolshiness. Bradshaw is homosexual, and said so during his interview. The Conservative candidate, Dr Adrian Rogers, was director of a body called the Conservative Family Institute and an unambiguous homophobe. The prospect of such a confrontation – not exactly 'on-message' in the Labour leadership's terms – seems to have attracted Exeter Labour activists still very bruised by London's handling of the Lloyd affair.

Although on the face of it this was an eminently winnable seat, Bradshaw was cautious, worried about the homophobic factor and the fact that the local party had been distracted from vital constituency work through 18 important months. As expected, Rogers concentrated on the gay issue. 'He was entirely negative and obsessed with what he calls family values,' Bradshaw says. Rogers repeatedly drew attention to Bradshaw's homosexuality, often using the formula that this was a 'disease-ridden, sterile and God-forsaken occupation'. In the final days of the campaign, Rogers issued a leaflet warning that in the event of a Bradshaw win 'schoolchildren would be in danger'.

Bradshaw found polling day an anxious affair and worked until the last minute drumming up votes. 'My agent was saying during the day he thought we would win by 3,000; I thought just three would do.' When he saw the exit polls after 10 p.m. he was sceptical, and he waited uneasily at Exeter Labour Club until 11.30 p.m. before going to the count. The result, expected at 1.30 a.m., didn't come for another two hours, and Bradshaw found it agony. The good news coming in from around the country didn't help: 'It just made the tension worse. I felt that if I didn't do as well here as people did elsewhere then everybody would point the finger,' he says. 'We were watching television but I just couldn't concentrate. Party workers kept coming up to me and saying: "Ben! Ben! Come down and look at your piles!" But I said no. I'm very cautious by nature. I psych myself up to expect the worst. There was something else, too. I wanted to win well, with a big swing, so that nobody could ever again say that being gay was an obstacle to success in public life. That was really important.'

He got his big win. The swing from Conservative to Labour was 12 per cent and Bradshaw finished with 29,000 votes to 18,000 for Rogers, an overwhelming victory. The winner crossed the stage and shook hands with all the losers, including Rogers. Then he went to the microphone and put the boot in. 'If this is a historic night for Britain it is a doubly historic night for Exeter, because the people here have not just rejected the Conservatives and chosen Labour, they've rejected fear and chosen hope, and they have rejected bigotry and chosen *reason*.' At this he punched the air and the crowd roared. 'And for that,' he added, as calm returned, 'I want to thank them from the depths of my heart.' He wasn't finished. 'I'd also like to thank the returning officer, the counters here in the hall, and the police. I'd like to thank the candidates from the Green Party, the old Liberal Party, the UK Independence Party and the Pensioners' Party for their clean and honourable campaign.' Nobody listening could fail to notice the absentees from that list: both the Conservatives and the Liberal Democrats. This winner didn't feel he had anything to be magnanimous about, and the loser wasn't very gracious either. After the BBC cut away, Rogers spoke in reply, declaring that this result was 'a nightmare for Exeter and a nightmare for Britain'. He was then drowned out by the crowd.

In a nice moment of contrast, Bradshaw had been thanking his partner at the moment the cameras cut away, and the next thing we saw on our screens was the scene at Huntingdon, where John Major and *his* partner, Norma, were going up to the stage to hear by how much he had won. In 1992 the Prime Minister's national triumph had been crowned by his local electorate with the largest majority in the country: 36,000. Alas, boundary

12. Ben Bradshaw (left) shakes the hand of Adrian Rogers, his Tory rival.

changes had moved half of his supporters elsewhere so there
would be no repetition of that; but still, even in 1997, he was
safe enough.

Major it was who had chosen May Day (or Mayday, or
International Labour Day) for the election. It was, in practical
terms, the last possible date in his mandate – the thinking owed
something to D:Ream (things can only get better) and something
to Micawber. In economic terms things did get better, but nobody
seemed to notice. And nothing turned up, no *deus ex machina*, no
Labour cock-up, no world crisis to frighten people into caution.
Major also chose a long campaign of six weeks instead of the
usual three or four, but again it did no good: after an initial
flurry of activity from the tabloids, emptying their cupboards of
Tory kiss-and-tell sagas, it settled into a dispiriting pattern. Like
those tennis players who stay rooted to the baseline swatting
back safe returns and relying on their opponents to make mistakes, Labour and the Tories took few risks and showed little
flair. Major made just one dash to the net, giving a personal
party election broadcast to say that only he could be trusted
to negotiate with Britain's European partners; but, as ever, it
appeared to have more to do with internal party politics than
with national ones. The last day of the campaign found the Prime
Minister still far behind in the polls, braving a hail of eggs in
supposedly marginal Stevenage.

Now he stood on the platform before a blue curtain adorned
with the word 'Huntingdonshire' while the High Sheriff of Cambridgeshire read the figures. Major received 31,500 votes and his
nearest rival (Labour) 13,000. The swing to Labour was 7 per
cent, so by the standards of the night this was a personal triumph
for the Conservative candidate. He thanked the usual people
with unusual warmth and went on: 'I'd like also, if I may, to
thank a number of people to whom I owe almost more than it's

possible to express readily and easily. Perhaps I may start with my agent, Peter Brown, a peer amongst agents. Not only my agent but a very old and dear friend . . . Above all, though, I would like to express my thanks to Norma, and to my family. Perhaps these things are most appropriately expressed in private, but I think most people who have known Norma, those people who have seen her, will realize that not only has she graced this constituency for 18 years, but I think she has graced a much larger stage in recent years, and my debt to her is one not easily paid.' This was eagerly applauded, and Norma bit her lip a couple of times. Her expression said that she would not miss this business of gracing stages everywhere.

'It is perfectly clear now,' Major continued, 'that the Labour Party have had an extremely successful evening. I telephoned Mr Blair a little over an hour ago to congratulate him on his success and to wish him good fortune in the great responsibilities that he will have in the years that lie ahead. This is a great country. He inherits a country in extremely good economic shape. I wish him every success in sustaining that in the interests of all the people of this country. I think I can promise that the Conservative Party will be a vigorous opposition. Where it is appropriate to support we will support; where it is in the interests of the country to support, we will support; where we believe the policies are wrong we will oppose vigorously, but honestly and fairly. But all that, I think, lies ahead for another day. For today let me perhaps just add one further thought. Elections always have winners and they always have losers. It is a very great occasion to win an election; it is a very great occasion to be elected to parliament. Many colleagues and old friends of mine will have contested seats tonight and lost them. Many colleagues will have contested seats on behalf of my party this evening, contested them well and bravely, but lost them. I would like to express to all of them my thanks for all that they've done on behalf of their country and my party, and my thanks also to the literally hundreds of thousands of people who have helped in the Conservative Party campaign, and the millions of our fellow-citizens who voted for the Conservative Party on this occasion.

'We are a great and historic party, the Conservative Party; we have had great victories in our time; we have had defeats in our time. We accept them both, I hope, with a certain dignity and a certain grace. Tonight we have been comprehensively defeated. We will listen to the voice of the electorate; we will consider what has been said to us. I think we must reflect upon it. I know that we will. And I know that when we have reflected upon it we will begin to prepare once again for that day in the future, I hope not too far distant, when my party may once again return to government in the service of this country. Thank you.'

In exchanges at the dispatch box, or when he indulged in rhetoric, John Major sounded grating and unconvincing; the conversational Major was always more plausible and attractive. Here he never attempted to raise his voice or score a point, and he produced a fine speech which made no excuses for what had happened but which still offered his followers consolation and a little hope. He did not say whether or when he would step down as party leader, but his tone and words suggested detachment. '*I think* we must reflect . . .' and '*I know that* when we have reflected . . .' did not seem to be the words of a man determined to give leadership. Above all, however, he showed that he was not personally broken by this huge defeat and that even he, as the man who had led his party into it, was capable of a certain dignity and a certain grace.

Michael Heseltine, whose 'friends and associates' had earlier been so fulsome about his own leadership qualities, now popped

13. John Major is consoled after leading his party to its worst defeat in 91 years.

up in person to stress his loyalty to Major. Asked about the role of sleaze in the defeat, he fought shy but finally observed with some accuracy: 'It's very difficult to think of a prime minister who has had so many examples of bad luck.' Another leadership contender was Stephen Dorrell, the Health Secretary, who was standing in the new Midlands seat of Charnwood. From there the BBC's Fergus Walsh reported that 'sources very close to Mr Dorrell are saying there should be a leadership election in July, that Mr Major should stay on for the moment'. Such a delay would be consistent with party rules, Walsh explained, but its true purpose would be to give Dorrell time to group his supporters and catch up with the likes of John Redwood. We got an idea who these sources close to the Health Secretary might be from

Walsh's next sentence: 'But Mr Dorrell was saying also – or Mr Dorrell's sources rather – that what we need to do is analyse what went wrong.' Oops.

One man not hiding behind 'friends' or 'sources' was the newly returned member for Old Bexley and Sidcup, Old Sir Edward Heath. Three months short of his 81st birthday, Sir Ted sat before the camera completely motionless apart from his lips and gave us his thoughts on what had gone wrong. 'In some cases we were out of touch with people and we were also pursuing policies which they didn't accept.' He then referred to one policy which no one else had mentioned all evening: 'I think myself that to put forward a complicated pensions scheme a fortnight before the campaign began was unwise. It's difficult for people to understand, and they immediately became worried about it, as elderly people do.'

It wasn't *all* bad news and backstabbing for the Conservatives. Peter Lilley, another potential leadership challenger, was re-elected in his new constituency of Hitchin and Harpenden, having fled there from marginal St Albans in what became known as a 'chicken run'. John Gummer was also safely back, and so was Michael Howard. Howard's defeat had been trailed as an outside chance all evening – he had been the 12th of Snow's original Dicey Dozen – and, had it happened, it would undoubtedly have broken the Festival Hall scream-ometer. Folkestone and Hythe was 47th on the LibDem target list and 300th on the Labour list, and if the voters there had followed the tactical pattern seen elsewhere this very unpopular Home Secretary would have been out. But they didn't. Howard's vote fell from 27,000 to 20,000, but the LibDems slipped from 18,500 to 14,000. It was Labour that gained, from 6,000 to 13,000, and the split vote let Howard through. For some reason, however, when he appeared on screen he looked more like a man who had lost a close relative than one who was rejoicing in a lucky escape. It was, he said, a dark night for the Conservative Party.

Peter Snow showed us the swings region by region. Seven per cent to Labour in Scotland and Wales; 10 per cent in the North of England; 11 per cent in the Midlands and the South, and 14 per cent in London. It seemed that wherever there were most Tories, the swing was biggest. 'When we look at our targets and see how good Tony Blair's party's aim has been, it's been *absolutely devastating*,' Snow said. And gee, it was time to strap ourselves in for another flyaround! There they were again, the blue blocks all over the country, and here we were swooping in from the south-west. 'The first one we're going for is Plymouth Sutton, then Exeter you can see just beyond it.' Pow! Pow! The blue blocks splintered into nothing and great red towers shot up in their place. 'There goes Exeter! Here comes Portsmouth North, the most difficult of those targets to hit!' Pow! Pow-powpow! In a trice we reached London and there were too many pows to count; 'huge Labour skyscrapers' thrusting up in dense formation, like a red Manhattan. Snow could not keep up and in no time we swept up through the Midlands in a shower of blue shards, and back and forth across the North, pow-powpowpow! This wasn't the Dambusters any more; it was carpet bombing. 'Just devastation everywhere.' Of the top 100 targets Labour had captured 83 so far and missed only two, Ceredigion and the London seat of Southwark North and Bermondsey.

This last was the seat of the LibDem Simon Hughes, who hung on but saw his majority clipped from 7,000 to 3,000. In the worst mistake of the evening, ITV had earlier announced with absolute confidence that Hughes was defeated, and Jonathan Dimbleby had to perform a little grovel. This was ITV being caught out in its rush to have results first; it did not always wait for the returning officer to speak. Elsewhere the LibDems were doing well. Colchester, Somerton and Frome and Hereford went from blue to yellow. Christchurch, like Eastleigh one of their spectacular by-election captures, slipped back to the Conservatives but, astonishingly, Newbury did not. Won by David Rendel in 1993, it stayed comfortably in the Liberal Democrat fold with a majority of 8,500. In south-west London they took two more seats, Richmond Park and Kingston and Surbiton, to take their tally in the capital to six. Richmond Park had since 1983 been the constituency of Jeremy Hanley, briefly and notoriously the Conservative Party Chairman (and thus a Cabinet Minister) under John Major. Hanley had done well to hold off the challenge of the LibDems' Jenny Tonge in 1992, but this time she beat him by 3,000 votes. Kingston saw several recounts, ending with a LibDem win by just 56 votes. For once they were getting the rub of the green.

Still the Labour gains rolled in. Inverness East, Nairn and Lochaber, all one seat and target number 25, was taken from the Liberal Democrats, while from the Tories came some more shire towns. Worcester (39) had been the subject of a lot of pre-election journalism because someone on the Conservative side identified 'Worcester woman' as the 'Basildon man' of 1997. 'A lot of nonsense, really,' said David Dimbleby – Labour got just over half the vote in Worcester and a majority of 7,500. Stafford (78) and Chester (27) followed in short order. Chester, never previously held by Labour, had for five years been the seat of the know-it-all television personality Gyles Brandreth. One of the effects of the 1992 election had been to remove him from our screens; perhaps now he would be back.

It was 4 a.m.: 529 of the 641 British seats had declared: Labour had won 379, the Conservatives 97 and the LibDems 32. ITV were predicting a Labour majority of 185 and the BBC were saying 187. Clement Attlee's great victory in 1945, for two generations the high-water mark of Labour fortunes, was going to be surpassed.

CHAPTER SEVEN

4 a.m. to 5 a.m.

*Attlee – a family connection – Evans ejected
– another Cabinet Minister – the map transformed –
sugar on Air Blair – a decorous party – Tory
plight – stonewall Howard – crumbs of comfort –
chicken runs – Mawhinney.*

For a small man, Attlee cast a long shadow. Of course he never expected to win in 1945 – Churchill had told the King the Conservatives would be back with a majority of at least 30 and Attlee believed the old man was right. On that occasion there was no night-time vigil for the results because a three-week delay had been allowed after polling day so that ballots could be collected from servicemen and women stationed around the world. Counting started first thing in the morning of 26 July and signs of a landslide were emerging by 10 a.m., just as Churchill was getting into his bath. By lunchtime, Labour had gained 100 seats and at 7 p.m. the Prime Minister tendered his resignation to the King. The final tally, to the utter astonishment of the country and the world, showed a Labour majority over all other parties in the House of Commons of 146. Attlee, who had begun the day with a family breakfast at his home in Stanmore at which the possibility of victory wasn't even mentioned, finished it as Labour Prime Minister at a celebration rally in Central Hall, Westminster, where he joined the crowd in an emotional rendition of 'England Arise'.

Over time, all this would acquire in Attlee's party the status of an Old Testament story, a fantastical episode to be read about and wondered at, but not perhaps taken too literally. That it ushered in the greatest of reforming governments and gave Labour its one truly inspiring period of achievement in power only added to its magical lustre. These were heroes; the party today had to live in the real world. And it was a long time ago – you had to be 73 years old in 1997 to have voted Labour back in 1945. There was simply no point in wondering if the party could ever do it again, indeed the idea was vaguely irreverent. And yet now, unbelievably, something similar *was* happening, and even the most sceptical and reserved of party activists were thrilled and amazed to see it and be part of it.

'I think I'd be a very hard man to please if I wasn't cheerful, Jonathan,' said Robin Cook when complimented on his seraphic smile. The Foreign Secretary-designate (who predicted a landslide during the campaign and was slapped down for it by the party's perception managers) had flown in from Edinburgh to join the Festival Hall celebrations. 'We have had tremendous support,' he said, 'and I have to say I find it both moving and humbling that the British people have put tremendous trust in us. We must now make sure that we repay that trust and that we do not abuse it in any way.' Was it daunting to face such responsibilities and challenges? 'It wouldn't be half so daunting, Jonathan, as the idea of going back into opposition for another five years. We welcome the challenge of office and we have been preparing for the challenge of office.'

Also jetting in for the party was Peter Mandelson, who told Francine Stock: 'I'm very, very happy, very relieved and very exhilarated, not just for all the people here, because they've done all the work, they've made this victory possible, but I'm very excited for the country obviously as well.'

'You are of course the architect . . .' Francine began, and he shook his head benignly.

'I'm one of them; I'm not the sole architect of anything.'

'What do you think was the particular point that caused such a dramatic victory?'

He knew the answer, and by now so did we: 'I think the main point was the creation of New Labour. You know, however awful the Tories are, and all their divisions, and their dogma and their drift [the third outing of the night for this triple-D] – and heaven knows the country wanted to shake them off a long time ago – but it took the creation of New Labour and the final transformation of the party after this long, ten-year struggle to remake ourselves, to clinch it. People felt they could trust the Labour Party again, we were safe; they could come home to us. And when that happened we were away.' With such a large majority, he was asked, was there not a risk that Labour too would be prone to divisions? 'Well, if there are little fissures appearing, I have every confidence that the BBC will be able to make them that little bit wider and create problems for ourselves.'

Mandelson has a personal link with the age of heroes, for his grandfather was Herbert Morrison, the Deputy Prime Minister under Attlee. As chairman of Labour's campaign committee in the 1945 election, Morrison could be said to have played the same part then as his grandson did in 1997, and among his many other achievements Morrison was also the power behind the Festival of Britain, for which the Festival Hall had been built. Stock asked whether the choice of this hall for this celebration owed something to the family connection, but Mandelson, as ever, had a point of his own to make: 'Well, I don't know whether, having managed this campaign, I'm going to exceed the majority gained by my grandfather when he managed the

Labour campaign in 1945. I think a little bit of family pride would encourage me to think we can get an even bigger majority than 1945. I don't know.'

This Mandelson–Morrison connection is striking, particularly as the two men have much else in common: like his grandson, Morrison made it his business to ensure that Labour was attractive to the middle classes and, like him, he had a knack for making enemies in his own party. But, as the historians say, such analogies should not be pressed too far. On the very day of Labour's triumph in 1945, for example, Morrison made a bid to become party leader and prime minister, and Attlee only pre-empted him by leaping into a car to the Palace and swiftly accepting the King's invitation to form a government. Back in the present, Mandelson promised there would be no surprises from New Labour. 'We have regained the trust of the British people and we're not going to betray them,' he said. The new government would be 'very responsible, very sober, our feet placed very firmly on the ground, but now ready to roll up our sleeves and get on with the job'.

The gains flowed in. Labour victory in Wirral South, first captured in a by-election a few months earlier, confirmed the obliteration of the Conservatives on Merseyside. When the election was called, four of the 16 seats there had been Tory; now all were Labour except Southport, gained by the LibDems. And Labour's Liverpool MPs included twin sisters: Angela Eagle, who had held Wallasey since 1992, and Maria, the winner in Garston.

The whole of the north-west used to be a sort of super-marginal in British elections, the swing region which in the 1970s and 1980s held the key to power. This was particularly true of the old textile towns in north Manchester and south Lancashire, which were the scene of some of the fiercest election campaigning.

Now there was scarcely a Tory to be seen. Bolton and Bury were entirely red, and Oldham, Rochdale and Wigan. Further north, Chorley had fallen and now it was joined by Ribble South, target number 87, and even Morecambe and Lunesdale (114) and Blackpool South (8), where Labour's winner was Gordon Marsden, editor of *History Today* magazine. With a recount under way in Lancaster and Wyre (111), it looked as though the Tories could be left with only two seats in the region, both of them mainly rural: Ribble Valley and Fylde.

In Yorkshire, Labour took Selby (88), while in the Midlands Edwina Currie duly met her fate in Derbyshire South (20), Labour's Mark Todd emerging from the contest there with a huge 14,000 majority. On either side of the West Midlands, the Wrekin (93) and Rugby and Kenilworth (124) joined the Labour fold, as did Corby (7) and, rather less predictably, Milton Keynes North East (163). In Welwyn Hatfield (72), on London's northern fringe, the small but stubborn form of David Evans was trying to hold back the red tide. A contract cleaning millionaire and the owner of Luton Town Football Club, Evans was a passionate Thatcherite who became a passionate Redwoodite, organizing Redwood's 1995 leadership challenge and coining his slogan: 'No Change; No Chance'. Evans can be blunt to the point of boorishness, as he demonstrated only weeks before the election when he observed to a class of sixth-formers in his constituency that his Labour rival, Melanie Johnson, 'had never done a proper job', was the mother of 'three bastard children', and 'did not have a hope in hell' of capturing his seat.

The BBC sent Anna Ford to cover this contest, and the effect was of a glorious computer dating cock-up: willowy feminine intellect meets jockey-sized male prejudice. She asked him if he expected to survive. 'It is Welwyn Hatfield and I like to think I'm not the normal Tory.' By which he meant? 'Say what I think.

Shoot from the hip.' As in those unfortunate remarks about Ms Johnson? 'I did upset a few people, but then some of what I said, people have said: you were right. Or else they said you shouldn't have said it but then they leant forward and said, "but we agree with you". So we'll find out in the next hour or so whether they did agree with me or not.' We did and they didn't. An 11 per cent swing was enough to give Johnson, a school inspector, a tidy majority of 5,500. Evans was out.

To the east of London, Chatham and Aylesford (148) completed Labour's control of the Thames Estuary seats, while Braintree in Essex dished out a defeat to another very senior Conservative, this time the most seasoned of all the outgoing members of the Cabinet, Tony Newton. Newton had managed to combine long service in government, mainly in health and social security ministries, with a low public profile, and as a result was neither popular nor unpopular among the public at large. In Westminster, by contrast, where for the past five years he had been Leader of the Commons, he had the rare distinction of being well liked and respected across the parties.

Newton had first won Braintree in the first election of 1974, and he built his majority to a peak of 17,500 in 1987, before seeing it slip back to 13,500 in 1992. Ranked 138 in Labour's target list, this was ostensibly almost as safe a seat as Jonathan Aitken's Thanet South, and safer than Sir Marcus Fox's Shipley. And, like them, it fell, this time on a swing of 13 per cent, which was enough to give Labour's Alan Hurst a majority of 1,500. 'Look at Tony Newton's face; the bleak knowledge that he has lost,' Jonathan Dimbleby commented. In truth, this cadaverous face was never a joyful one, but it did look even glummer than usual. Michael Brunson added: 'They say that all political careers end in tears; it is a particularly tearful atmosphere around Tony Newton.'

Tears or not, we had more history. As Anthony King had pointed out earlier, five of Churchill's Cabinet Ministers lost their seats in 1945; now six had gone in 1997: the Foreign Secretary, the President of the Board of Trade, the Defence Secretary, the Leader of the Commons, the Scottish Secretary and the Chief Secretary to the Treasury: Rifkind, Lang, Portillo, Newton, Forsyth and Waldegrave. It was an astonishing cull of men who for the most part could have expected, if they had survived, to remain in the upper reaches of Tory politics for another decade at least. Among former Cabinet Ministers under John Major there was also a high toll: Aitken, Mellor, Lamont, Hunt and Hanley. Lesser ministers, some of whom would confidently have expected to rise eventually to Cabinet rank, fared no better. Among the casualties were John Bowis, Sir Nicholas Bonsor, Alistair Burt, Tom Sackville, Ian Sproat, James Douglas-Hamilton, Rod Richards and Robin Squire. Far more than the usual quota of careers were ending in tears on this one night.

So great was the change that a studio graphic which usually doesn't work on election night came into its own. A map of Britain coloured as appropriate in blue, red and yellow may seem an obvious device for illustrating change, but it suffers from two drawbacks. First, Labour seats are predominantly urban and thus small, while the Conservatives dominate in the big country seats. Thus you could have a large advantage to Labour while the map gave the impression that the country was still overwhelmingly Tory. Secondly, too few seats normally change hands for the difference between before and after to be obvious at a glance. This time, however, Peter Snow was able to show off the maps to considerable effect. Scotland, the north-east, Lancashire and the Thames Estuary were visibly redder; but the biggest change was in the centre: far more red now appeared in an area stretching from North Wales to the West Midlands and Northamptonshire, and up towards south Yorkshire and the Humber. Middle England, once a sea of blue, was now mainly red.

Flying in the darkness above this changing country was the Labour leader, on his way to join the festivities at the Festival Hall by private jet (there must have been a whole squadron of them in the service of the Labour Party on this night). And even here on Air Blair a camera was present to record the victor's progress. As soon as the plane touched down at Stansted, the footage was fed through to both channels and, perhaps unsurprisingly, ITV liked it the more. 'While Tony Blair was flying down to London,' Jonathan announced with a perky grin, 'we had a camera inside there and I'm told that there were some very interesting things happening on that plane. So let's have a look at what it was.'

There was Tony in shirtsleeves, in a very big grey leather seat, with Alastair Campbell (who else?) facing him from another. The leader smiled and laughed. 'This is real relaxation,' said Jonathan, although the man looked anything but relaxed and promptly asked for some papers to work on. 'This is the intimacy of power; it's not often that you will get, after this, that sort of access on a prime ministerial plane.' We heard a woman's voice asking Campbell: 'Finchley? Did you say *Finchley*?' The reply was a nod, and the leader looked up from his notes and grinned proudly. Finchley indeed. Then Blair asked somebody off-camera: 'Could you make sure, the moment we touch down, that I can speak to John Prescott?'

A tray of silverware came into view: tea. 'He's been surviving on tea during all this,' Brunson told us.

'Looks like an awful lot of milk going in there,' said Jonathan. And then: 'He also takes sugar in his tea!'

Sure enough, the silver tongs could clearly be seen dropping a single white cube into the leader's cup.

At this point self-awareness at last caught up with Jonathan, and he paused to explain: 'All these details will become immensely important once he becomes Prime Minister. Does he take sugar will be the question that everyone now has an answer to.' He went on: 'Of course he knows that the camera's there and I suspect that – he's a canny politician – when he said he wanted to speak to John Prescott, it wouldn't surprise me that *he wanted people to know* that he wanted to speak to John Prescott.'

But the *Hello TV* interlude was not over. Campbell gave up the seat facing the leader to a woman, and Tony put down his papers and chatted with her. It was Cherie. She reached out a hand and he took it and smiled.

'Aaahh,' breathed Brunson.

'That's the moment, isn't it?' said Jonathan in delight. '*That's* the moment. In the studio there's a lot of oohing and aahing as people watch that.' And some reaching for sickbags, no doubt.

At last Blair withdrew his hand and returned to his notes. 'She has been a tremendous help to him during the campaign,' said Brunson. 'One or two people wondered whether Cherie would take to political life. She was plainly rather tense about it all at the beginning, but [we glimpsed her smiling face] look at that! She's now going to be part of the team.'

The camera switched to Campbell, seated across the aisle looking rather tired, and Jonathan told us that this man was regarded by the media as 'the tough thug of the Labour Party'.

Brunson, by now awash with the milk of human kindness, leapt to Alastair's defence, insisting that he had mellowed of late and that 'incidentally, he'll take over a very, very large office in Downing Street'.

David Dimbleby, as you might expect, was not doing any of

this oohing and aahing that his little brother so relished. He was far brisker with the BBC cut of the flight footage – from which the hand-clasp and the sugar lump had been brutally excised. This was his voice-over: 'Tony Blair has been flying in to go to the party at the Festival Hall, with Cherie his wife, on the way down. Seems to be already at work. Cups of tea, not champagne. In fact the whole way that Labour has treated this so far, apart from occasional bursts of energy at the Festival Hall, and the Folletts' failure to open a bottle of champagne at Stevenage, has been rather muted, as though they'd been so well disciplined for the campaign, and so orderly, that now that they've got a victory on a huge scale, they're rather staggered by it. Alastair Campbell there, the press secretary, also sipping a cup of tea. [Did his tone imply this was unusual?] A serious moment, as they plan what they're going to do when they go to Number Ten . . . It's interesting that this spirit of rather modest determination through the campaign seems to have lasted. No exuberance, no sudden burst of energy.'

Muted, orderly, serious . . . what about all that relaxation and intimacy? Could this be the same Tony Blair, the same flight and the same camera? It was, but it certainly sounded very different. Were these Dimbleby boys separated at birth?

The Liberal Democrats by now were holding 35 seats, and they hadn't finished. Oxford West and Abingdon, lately the seat of the now-retired ex-Minister John Patten, swung by 10 per cent to the LibDems. Lewes followed suit, and so did some constituencies in the traditional Liberal heartland, the south-west. Cornwall South East, Tory since 1974, fell easily, as did West Devon and Torridge. The latter had been the seat of Emma Nicholson, the former Conservative Party Deputy Chairman who in 1996 crossed the floor to join the Liberal Democrats. She did not stand again but left the way clear for John Burnett, a solicitor and former Royal Marine, who was elected on a modest swing with a majority of 2,000. Nicholson's old constituency had thus followed her across the party divide.

ITV took us quickly to the Pizza on the Park, where Jackie Ashley reported: 'A huge cheer has just gone up here, Jonathan, and Emma Nicholson was absolutely jubilant, waving her arms in the air . . . People here are absolutely delighted with what's happening, not only for themselves, where the results are far exceeding expectations, but also with what Labour's doing as well . . . Huge cheers have been going up when the Tory Cabinet Ministers – William Waldegrave, Michael Portillo, Ian Lang – have lost their seats. I think perhaps the biggest cheer of the night, though, was when Martin Bell won in Tatton, because of course the Liberal Democrats and Labour stood down there for him. This is a victory against the Conservatives for Labour and the Liberal Democrats, who certainly on some things such as constitutional reform will be working together.'

Looking over her shoulder, Jonathan could see the party in progress, and he was not impressed. 'It's a somewhat more decorous affair in your restaurant there, than the extraordinary goings-on at the Festival Hall. Do you think that's just Lib-Demmery?'

Ashley wasn't sure: 'I think it's a smaller affair altogether, Jonathan. Certainly a good quantity of beer and wine is being drunk, and I've also seen some champagne . . . There's no music and there's no dancing, but I wouldn't really call it decorous.' The implication was that the LibDems were being indecorous, but in ways we couldn't see.

Alastair had another theory about why they appeared subdued: 'They can't quite believe what they've done.' Nationally, he explained, the LibDem share of the vote was actually down, 'and yet here we have it [pointing to a very yellow display]: this is their list of target seats and they've knocked off one, two, three, four, five, six, seven, eight, nine, ten, eleven, twelve, thirteen, *fourteen* of them.' Labour had taken a few and the Tories had held on to one or two, but 'the tribute to tactical voting and the targeting of those key seats is quite extraordinary, because also well beyond these seats they've taken Harrogate, Carshalton, Northavon, Sutton and Cheam, Sheffield Hallam, Richmond Park and they've also taken Kingston and Surbiton . . . So the national share of the vote may be down, but they have made 23 gains and we're still saying at the end of the day they'll have 46 seats in the House of Commons. An extraordinary result for the Liberal Democrats, Jonathan.'

A little later, Paddy Ashdown was stopped by reporters on his way into the pizza party and asked what he had expected. 'We thought we'd do better than you thought we'd do, but not as well as this.' A rousing welcome – 'We want Paddy!' – greeted him as he entered, and that tanned face was creased in the widest of smiles. Lord Holme, his campaign director, mounted a podium and thanked, not Paddy, but someone we had never heard of. 'Their host at the restaurant,' Jonathan explained, 'which we don't name because it would be advertising it, but it's famous.' (The BBC had no such scruples: 'They're at the Pizza on the Park,' David announced boldly.) Then up stepped the party leader, to prolonged applause. 'Richard, the whole of the campaign team, you have been *absolutely stunning*,' he said. 'I can't tell you what it's been like out there, and I know I speak for all my parliamentary colleagues – and there are now many more than there were before [cheers and whoops] – the way that you've fought this campaign, under the superb direction of Richard, who's done so stunningly for all of us, and now we have a lot of work to do. We are the largest force of Liberal Democrats and Liberals that this country has had since the days of Lloyd George [more cheers].' The absence of grammar in all this probably testified less to exhaustion than to emotion. Ashdown, who had become a grandfather during the campaign, had had a few very good weeks; his party was the party of disappointment no longer.

What of the party of government? The Conservatives were in shock, punch-drunk from defeat after defeat. They were heading for their smallest tally of MPs since 1906 and their lowest share of the vote since (thank you, David) 1832. No one, not even those who had really faced up to the possibility of life in opposition, could have imagined that they would do so on such terms – without Portillo, without seats in Scotland or Wales, trounced in London and the big cities; a genuine rump. There was no mistaking the anger in the voice of an electorate which had broken all its own rules to ensure what Jackie Ashley called a 'victory against the Conservatives'. Never before had there been tactical voting on this scale; never before had so many Tory voters stayed at home; never before had so many crossed directly to Labour. They had smiled on the doorsteps, but when they cast their vote they were vicious. Michael Dobbs's formula of 'time for change' could not begin to account for desertion on this scale. And it wasn't with pride but with bitterness towards an ungrateful nation that senior Tories kept pointing to the strength of the economy that Tony Blair would inherit.

In the BBC studio, the pundits saw these raw wounds and had a jolly good poke at them. 'What is there left to lead?' David Dimbleby asked Robin Oakley, who replied: 'The Tories are in an extraordinary state. Everybody we've spoken to tonight has said, "Well, we've got to regroup," but regroup as what? Do they regroup as a Euro-sceptic party when, for example, the

Liberal Democrats as the most pro-European party have had their most successful election ever? Do they regroup fighting devolution when they won't have a single Welsh or Scottish MP? They've got to really rethink their position from the start.' Who would win the leadership? Oakley thought the Euro-sceptics might be weakened and Heseltine's prospects had dimmed, but that young William Hague's chances had improved 'because it looks as though Labour will be there for a couple of terms'.

But Europe wasn't the only issue dividing the Tories, as Anthony King pointed out. 'One of the party tricks you could play if you want to is get two Conservatives in a room and ask them what they think about the fall of Margaret Thatcher back in 1990. One of them will think it is the end of civilization as we know it, and another will say, "Rejoice, rejoice, it was a wonderful occasion." Those kinds of ideological divisions are just as deep today as they were in the Labour Party in the 1970s and early '80s.'

Peter Kellner, dwelling for a moment on the wipe-out in the cities, had an even darker thought: 'Given that the Tories don't control the local government in these areas, and given that their membership is falling, it seems to me that Conservatives have a real problem in reconstructing themselves as a national party . . . All the things which create a functioning party at local level – having councillors, having MPs – that has ceased to exist in large parts of Britain, and in particular urban Britain. I think that will make it incredibly difficult for them to rebuild their base.'

Oakley and King had some further punishment to dish out. Oakley thought the mood of 'time for change' had been around for years, but that the repeated scandals had given it powerful new force. 'Sleaze and the way it accumulated through this parliament fed into the whole idea of a tired old administration whose standards were slipping,' he said. King, who is a member of the Nolan Committee on standards in public life, was more sweeping: 'The core fact is that this government, over time, earned the contempt of the majority of the British people for the way it governed the economy in the first few years, for the sleaze that we've heard about several times tonight, for its disunity over Europe. And it also, I think, caused an awful lot of people to want to wreak revenge on the Conservative Party.'

On ITV, John Suchet was standing outside Conservative Central Office on the pavement in Smith Square. This was the place where on past election nights admiring crowds would cheer and sing as Margaret Thatcher waved from the window above – but now Suchet had only a couple of security men for company. 'They may be dancing to D:Ream at the Festival Hall,' he said, 'but here it's a very different story.' John Major was on his way here from Huntingdon by road and other senior party figures had been arriving. Lord Cranborne, Tory leader in the Lords, shook his head on the way in and said: 'Absolutely dreadful result. Dreadful result.' Maurice Saatchi, the party's favourite ad-man, had no message for anyone. And Suchet reported: 'I am told by a very senior source that Lady Thatcher, although not in this building at the moment, has been watching the results come in overnight. She's said to be *absolutely devastated*.'

Time for a Paxman moment. Jeremy had had a quiet couple of hours while the results tumbled in, all the drama and spilt blood rendering his particular form of entertainment superfluous. There had been just one moment of fun: a brief exchange with the beaten Michael Portillo who suddenly realized he no longer had to play these games and simply said: 'Oh Jeremy, stop this nonsense.' Michael Howard, still an MP after beating the odds in Folkestone, did not have the luxury of simply switching off

4 a.m. to 5 a.m.

like that. His gloomy countenance now loomed up from deepest Kent, and Jeremy launched one of his well-polished pseudo-questions: 'Mr Howard, what does it feel like to be part of an endangered species?' There could be no answer to that, of course, so Howard fell back on the tested: 'It is a dark night for the Conservative Party.' There ensued a delightful exchange:

PAXMAN: What will you tell the Prime Minister tomorrow about how long he should stay leading the party?

HOWARD: I have always supported John Major. I will continue to support him for as long as he wishes to remain leader of the party.

PAXMAN: So you won't stand for the leadership?

HOWARD: I will support John Major for as long as he wishes to remain leader of the Conservative Party.

PAXMAN: So if there were a vacancy you would stand for it.

HOWARD: There is no vacancy [small smile] and I repeat, Jeremy, that I will support John Major for as long as he wishes to remain leader of the party.

Paxman, leaning over the rail of his balcony and talking to the tellywall, adopted his most jaundiced air; this was too wearying. He tried again: 'There will be a vacancy, perhaps jolly soon. Will you stand for it?' Howard: 'There is no vacancy at the moment and, as I say, I will support John Major for as long as he wishes to remain our leader.' Paxman: 'After that all bets are off?' Howard: 'There's no vacancy at the moment.'

If time had permitted, no doubt Jeremy would have found a dozen more ways of framing the same question, and Howard would have repeated his response a dozen more times, with equal patience. Alas we had to move on, to questions about the past (too soon to rake over it) and the future (too soon to think about it). And then it was good-night. Very illuminating, as Jeremy would say.

*

For the Tories, though, it seemed that the worst might be over at last. A handful of important seats, some of which, on the evidence of the earlier swings, might have fallen, now came up Tory again. Gillian Shephard, who had been very anxious in Norfolk South West (Labour target 162), won with 2,500 votes to spare even though those *Observer* pollsters had tipped her to lose. In neighbouring Norfolk South (205) the former Cabinet Minister John MacGregor also returned without trouble. Despite a swing of nearly 18 per cent, Teresa Gorman kept her seat at Billericay (221), but her majority was down from 21,000 to 1,300. Michael Heseltine was safely returned at Henley and issued a defiant rallying cry: 'I was first elected to parliament in 1966. It was a Labour landslide and people spent a great deal of time and trouble worrying about the future of the Tory Party. Four years later we were back. See you around.' Douglas Hogg was re-elected in Grantham despite all his BSE woes, and so was Sir Nicholas Lyell, one of the villains of the Matrix Churchill affair. At the same time a stream of shire and commuter-belt results, so long delayed by the extraction of those local election ballot papers, flowed in at last to give a reassuring blue hue to the bottom of the screen: Banbury, Chichester, Aldershot, Bracknell, Surrey East, Vale of York, Chipping Barnet, Chelmsford West. There was, after all, a part of England they could still call their own.

Several ministers who joined the 'chicken run' from threatened seats to safer ones now saw the manoeuvre pay off. Stephen Dorrell's old constituency of Loughborough (target 45) fell to Labour, while his new seat of Charnwood (224) returned him with a majority of 6,000. Sir George Young had swapped Ealing, Acton and Shepherd's Bush (all one seat, and presented to Labour by the boundary commissioners) for the safer pastures of Hampshire North West (290), and emerged with a majority of 11,500.

One who was less fortunate was John Watts, who left Slough after boundary changes gave Labour a notional majority there of 50 and chose instead to fight Reading East (123), the former seat of the veteran Tory, Sir Gerard Vaughan, which had a notional majority of 10,500. The Reading voters also decided it was time for a change, and they elected Labour's Jane Griffiths instead of Watts.

The most famous of the chicken runners was Brian Mawhinney, the Conservative Party Chairman and a Cabinet member, who left Peterborough after 18 years following some unfavourable boundary changes which elevated it to Labour target number 73. While he was still the city's MP, Mawhinney used occasionally to regale the nation with his accounts of what the man and woman in the Peterborough pub were talking about – never sleaze or Europe, for example, but more often the wonders of Mr Major's economic boom and Britain's influential position in the world. Once the combative Ulsterman decided to move on, however, it seems that conversation in Peterborough pubs took a different turn, for the city elected Labour's Helen Brinton with a majority of 7,000.

Mawhinney, meanwhile, won his new seat of Cambridgeshire North West comfortably, although, when he appeared at the declaration, 'comfortable' was not a word that sprang to mind. Heseltine had been on and off TV all night making the best of things, but since 11 p.m. nothing at all had been seen of Mawhinney, the garrulous Party Chairman and dynamic campaign mastermind. He could not, however, avoid speaking at his own constituency declaration; when he finally emerged there, he was like a zombie, his face a ghostly grey and his delivery halting. Labour, he said, 'have done well . . . and we have not done well . . . and we will need to reflect on that and the lessons that emerge from it in the days that lie ahead . . . But that *is* for the days that lie ahead . . . In the meantime there is a job to be done . . . Thank you . . . for giving me the honour of doing it.' A little later he appeared on BBC for an interview looking a bit healthier, but scarcely had he opened his mouth to speak than the producers cut away to the Festival Hall and yet another chorus of 'Things Can Only Get Better'.

CHAPTER EIGHT

After 5 a.m.

Blair's progress – a former leader – change of shirt –
South Bank speech – a crystal vase – OK we lost – silver
for Coe – Freeman falls – time for bed – coronation
march – Sinn Fein's gains – Winchester two – final figures.

With 600 seats declared out of 659, Labour was on course for a total of about 420 seats and an overall majority of around 180; the Liberal Democrats were set to take about 45 and the Conservatives, who had won 336 seats in 1992, were expected to finish the 1997 election with fewer than half that number: about 165. Since one-third of the undeclared seats were in Northern Ireland, which prefers to count its votes in daylight, and only a few of the remainder were what now qualified as marginals, just a handful of unlucky people were still on tenter-hooks. For the rest, it was all over bar the shouting, the dancing and the formalities. Of shouting and dancing there was to be plenty, while the formalities held an unusual excitement and importance. Those last results, moreover, brought surprises fully in keeping with the dramas that preceded them.

We first glimpsed Tony Blair long ago at 11.30 p.m., through the thoughtfully parted curtains of his home in County Durham. He went from there to his declaration at Newton Aycliffe, and thence to Trimdon Labour Club. After a second speech, to local party loyalists, it was off to Teesside and quickly by air down to Stansted. Now he was on the road into central London and the Royal Festival Hall, where the crowd, the cameras and the music had moved outside to await his triumphal entry. Crowd barriers were in place and a stage was ready for his appearance before this audience of party workers, invited guests and, further back, impromptu arrivals attaching themselves to the celebrations. At one barrier, by the foot of the steps up to the stage, stood Neil Kinnock and Peter Mandelson, and behind them John Prescott, his wife Pauline, and Robin Cook. Gordon Brown was not on parade.

Kinnock had been around all night, having performed a relaxed and amiable turn in Paxman's gallery on BBC before showing up at the party all smiles and hugs. Jeremy had asked him the obvious but necessary question: did he feel just a hint of envy? He would not be human, he replied, if he did not. But he was full of graciousness and generosity, remarking in particular on how well Peter Mandelson had done. Maybe, he suggested philosophically, the country had needed the extra five years since 1992 to learn to trust Labour and to distrust the Tories, whose divisions had been their undoing. 'The Conservative Party,' he said, 'has given the impression that it takes itself more seriously than it takes the country. We, for a short period, gave that impression; we've been paying the price ever since.'

As D:Ream pumped out their song over the South Bank again and again, the man who led the Labour Party through nine of its most difficult years now stood, beaming and laughing in the limelight, blowing kisses or winking to familiar faces in the crowd and tapping his hand merrily in time with the music. Mandelson clapped along, and so did Pauline Prescott. John Prescott, about to become Deputy Prime Minister, stood expressionless in the middle. Around them the crowd danced, sang and waved while television cameras swooped and panned. Even David Dimbleby managed to be slightly impressed. 'That looks a bit sparkier than the scenes we saw before,' he said. 'Atmosphere building up as we await Tony Blair's arrival . . . You can sense the feeling of exuberance and relief after the struggle to win this election, after the past 18 years . . . At the beginning of this campaign all these people working for the party were so uncertain and nervous and tense lest it go wrong, and then to discover that not only has it not gone wrong, but it's exceeded their wildest dreams . . . No wonder they're exuberant.'

On ITV, Jonathan Dimbleby was also watching the crowd, also building us up. 'This is the face of New Labour,' he said. 'All ages, different nationalities, races, sexes. A mixture of people. You would not know what party they came from, it's a complete cross-section.'

Brunson joined in: 'Look at them, everybody enjoying themselves. Now *where's* Tony Blair?'

Jonathan: 'Tony Blair's keeping them waiting at the moment. It's probably been meticulously timed. None of this is haphazard.'

Alastair Stewart agreed, observing that it was eerily similar to a Clinton election event. Stewart had covered the 1992 American election and he recalled the same kind of 'stage management' in Little Rock, Arkansas, on the day of Bill Clinton's first victory: 'The way everybody queued up and waited and they were corralled there. And the moment he burst on to the stage with Hillary was, I suspect, precisely what we are going to see in a few moments.'

And then Jonathan had another revelation with a Clinton flavour: 'We're told that he [Blair] went back to change his shirt . . . You can't blame him. He's been wearing the same shirt probably a lot of the day and certainly a lot of the evening and it's very hot. Some of *us* would like to change a shirt, but we'll get our chance later.'

Occasionally there would be a pause in the D:Ream stream and anticipation would rise. Early trains in and out of Charing Cross station rumbled over Hungerford bridge, and one engine driver toot-tooted to the crowd. They cheered, perhaps in reply or perhaps because they thought this heralded the arrival of the leader's car. Unnoticed at this late stage, Blackpool North and Fleetwood declared. It was target 75 and it was won by Labour's Joan Humble with a majority of 9,000 votes. Both the north and south divisions of another eternally Tory town had changed hands; the landladies, it seemed, now preferred Labour.

At last David Dimbleby announced: 'There is the sign of a rather grand motor car arriving, which may be Mr Blair. I think it is.' The rather grand motor car stopped and out stepped the leader, suited security men around him scanning the crowd. Tom Sawyer, the Labour General Secretary and formally the host at this celebration, greeted him, and then Blair headed off down the crowd barriers, shaking hands warmly, two or three at a time, and falling once into a vice-like hug out of which he had to prise himself. Eventually he reached the line-up of party VIPs and there he gave a warm hug to Neil Kinnock, whose lips appeared to form the words: 'Much better than last time! Brilliant!' Up on to the stage Blair strode, with Cherie behind passing him those speech notes he had studied in the plane. On either side red banners said: 'New Labour', while above now a yellow screen displayed the words: 'New government.' All around was a cacophony of noise. 'To-ny! To-ny! To-ny! To-ny!'

'Thank you! Thank you!' he shouted several times, waiting for calm, and then, with a glance up at the lightening sky: 'A new dawn has broken, has it not? And it is wonderful.' They loved it. 'We always said that if we had the courage to change, then we could do it, and we did it.' They cheered to the echo. 'Let me say this to you: the British people have put their trust in us. It is a moving and it is a humbling experience. And the size of our likely majority now imposes a special sort of responsibility upon us. We have been elected as New Labour and we will govern as New Labour. We were elected because as a party today we represent the whole of this nation. And we will govern for the whole of this nation – every single part of it. We will speak up for that decent, hard-working majority of the British people whose voice has been silent for all too long in our political life.' Every one of these sentences was cheered and applauded. 'And we'll set about doing the good, practical things that need to be done in this country – extending educational opportunity not to an elite but to all our children; modernizing our welfare state, rebuilding our National Health Service as a proper National Health Service to serve the needs of Britain. We will work with business to create that dynamic and enterprising economy we need. And we will work with all our people for that just and decent society that the British people have wanted for so long.

'This vote tonight has been a vote for the future, for a new era of politics in Britain, so that we can put behind us the battles of this past century and address the battles of the new century. It will be a Britain renewed, where through education and technology and enterprise we equip our country for the future in a different and new economic world. And where we build a nation united. With common purpose, shared values, with no one shut out, no one excluded, no one told that they do not matter. In that society, tolerance and respect will be the order of the day, as we watch our children grow in strength and our elderly rest easy and secure in old age. That is the country we have wanted for so long. A Britain whose politics start once again to live up to the finest ideals of public service. And a Britain that stands tall in the world, whose sense of its future is as certain and confident as its sense of its own history.

'Today, on the eve of this new millennium, the British people have ushered in this new era of politics, and the great thing about it is that we have won support in this election from all walks of life, from all classes of people, from every single corner of our country. We are now today the People's Party. The party of all the people, the many not the few, the party that belongs to every part of Britain, no matter what people's background, or their creed, or their colour. The party that can stand up for what is a great country. We want everyone to feel proud in their country tonight because they all have a stake in its success. I believe in Britain and tonight the people of Britain are uniting behind New Labour. They are uniting around basic British values, uniting to put the divisions of the past behind us, uniting to face the challenges of the future, uniting at long last as one nation.

'Three days ago, I quoted one of my predecessors, John Smith. He said, "All we ask is the chance to serve." [The mention of Smith brought applause.] Tonight the British people have given us the chance to serve, and serve we will, with all our heart and all our mind. And to you, all of you that have come here this evening, I say thank you for all your work and for all your help. It's been a long journey for this party, has it not? It's been a long journey. I'm delighted that Neil Kinnock is here tonight with us. [Cheers, and a very moved Kinnock nodded to acknowledge long applause.] Neil took us back from the brink of extinction and helped make this party what it is today. And it is with real pride that all of us here today, young and old, from every part of the country, from every background, we say tonight, the British people have given us the chance to serve you; you have put your trust in us. We shall repay that trust for you; we govern for you. Finally, all these years we have been people saying, but never given the chance to do. The only purpose in being in politics is to do, to get things done, to make things happen. Now we have the chance to make things happen, and we take that responsibility upon us and we say we shall discharge it. And we shall make this country as proud of us as tonight we are proud of them. Thank you very much indeed.'

The Dimblebys, as usual, were divided in their views. This was Jonathan: 'So, Tony Blair with a revivalist, visionary speech, a speech with passion, directed not only at his audience there, but to the wider audience.' And this was David: 'A speech which he has made many times before on the stumps, slightly revamped for this victory moment. Not an emotional speech, thanking all the supporters and party workers who have gathered there, but a restatement of policy and intention . . .' It was, David added, 'a slightly stilted way of dealing with a victory party', and 'not at all what you would expect'.

Both of them, in their ways, were right. Where the Sedgefield declaration speech at midnight had been an intimate affair, meant for a small audience there and for television viewers in living-rooms elsewhere, this was delivered in hustings style, the *appassionato* mixed in due proportion with the *piano*. When Tony Blair does that, there is an unmistakable echo of the pulpit in his voice, and 'revivalist' is a good word for it. It was true at the same time that the content was not aimed at the Labour faithful on the South Bank (who would probably at that moment have cheered random extracts from the Argos catalogue); it was not a speech of celebration or of shared emotion. He was still talking to the whole country. In fact that word, 'country', appears in the speech six times, the word 'nation' four times, the word 'people' 11 times and the words 'Britain' or 'British' 14 times. From the crowd, the most heartfelt expressions of enthusiasm came when Blair mentioned John Smith and Neil Kinnock, and, had the leader spared a word for Keir Hardie or Clem Attlee, there would not have been a dry eye in the house; but that is not his way. He wanted and wants, as he said, 'to put behind us the battles of the past century'.

Robin Oakley observed: 'Mr Blair was very conscious that he was speaking to the nation outside, as well as to his own party.' To which David Dimbleby snorted: 'What? At half-past five in the morning? Come on, pull the other one.' But Oakley stuck to his guns. 'The whole Labour campaign has been one of careful reassurance. Remember that image that Roy Jenkins produced at the beginning of the campaign. There was Mr Blair carrying this precious crystal vase along a long, slippery corridor. Well, he got there, to the end of the corridor, with the vase, and he didn't even dare to do a little pirouette there with it still in his hands.' Tony Blair still felt the need to reassure.

By now Blair and Prescott, looking very like Clinton and Gore, were shaking hands along the crowd barrier again, followed by Cherie, Pauline and the rest. D:Ream were back in action and the sky no longer wore the grey of dawn but the cheerful blue of another beautiful May day. Eventually they moved inside, where Blair made his fourth and briefest speech of the night direct to party workers, praising them as 'the most magnificent, professional, disciplined force in British politics' and then reminding them of the weight of responsibility now falling on the party.

At about that moment a van from north London was crossing the Thames and approaching the Festival Hall. It was decked with Labour posters bearing the name 'Stephen Twigg' and on board was the victorious candidate for Enfield Southgate himself. 'As we got closer we saw people who were leaving the party,' Twigg remembers. 'I could see them spotting my name on the posters and thinking. I could see them turning to each other and their lips making the word 'Portillo'. When we arrived I was mobbed. It was a bit like being one of the Spice Girls for an

14. Stephen Twigg makes his entrance at the Festival Hall party.

evening. Cherie was really nice and Tony Blair asked me: "Did you do it? Did you really do it?" It was the most emotional experience of my life.'

John Major arrived in Smith Square just as Tony Blair finished speaking on the South Bank. He marched swiftly from car to door, past the Press, as one reporter shouted after him: 'Will you now resign? Will you now resign?' The cameras were inside already to witness a brave and enthusiastic welcome from party workers and from a handful of well-known Tory figures, including William Hague and Michael Portillo. The Prime Minister climbed a few stairs to a little landing and turned around to speak. In the hush, someone shouted: 'John Major, you're a star,' and there was more applause. He looked the same as ever, neither tired nor despondent, and he communicated his particular type of cheerfulness to his party staff. They had done well and made sacrifices, and it was all very disappointing. 'I don't think there was much that we left undone that we could have done. There are some times in politics when the ball just rolls in the opposite direction and there isn't a great deal you can do about it.' At such moments, he said, 'you just step back, ask yourself why you didn't win, and put yourself in a position to make sure that next time you get it right, and you do win'. The Conservative Party was a great and by any standards a successful organization which had transformed the country over 18 years, and it would return to government. Some of those who had lost their seats – and he looked at Portillo – would undoubtedly be back. 'There is something in the Conservative philosophy and the Conservative instinct,' he said, 'that runs absolutely with the grain of the British instinct.'

He paid tribute to the party organization, to friends at party head office and to Norma, and then he drew a deep breath and smiled. 'So, right! OK! We lost!' he said, and they all laughed. 'So go away for the weekend, relax, fire yourselves up again and then come back. When you come back at the beginning of next week we've got a job and we'd better start doing it.'

From there ITV switched to Alastair Stewart and his battle-ground. There, spread out across the wall, were the columns of Labour targets, each a dozen deep beneath the percentage swing figure needed to capture them. Six columns could fit on the wide screen and we could see everything from 0 per cent to 5 per cent. All but one of those had turned red, the exception being Falmouth and Camborne down in Cornwall, which had yet to declare. Otherwise it was red, red, red. Next Stewart displayed the columns from 6 per cent to 11 per cent. Here there was a smattering of blue (including a conspicuous error: in the 6 per cent column

Colne Valley was given as a Tory hold although Labour had taken it with a 5,000-vote majority). The highest-ranked seat Labour had failed to gain was Colchester in the 8 per cent column, which was taken instead by the LibDems. The best Conservative performance of the night, by this measure, was at Bury St Edmunds in the 9 per cent column, which was held by just 368 votes. In the 10 per cent column only two seats were still Tory, Aldridge-Brownhills and Eddisbury, with two more, Kettering and Lichfield, still to declare. There were two again in the 11 per cent column. It was only in the 12 per cents that the Conservatives managed to hold on to most of the seats.

No matter how you looked at it, this was an asteroid impact. Not only were the Conservatives absent from Scotland and Wales, they had lost more than half their seats in the south-west and the Welsh border country, while in the north they were thoroughly rusticated. If you drew a line from the Humber to the Mersey and took the whole, huge region from there to the Scottish border, the Conservatives had held nearly 40 seats there before the election. Now they held 12. In Kent, Labour began the night without a single seat; now they had eight, or half the county. And not only had the Tories been devastated in the big metropolitan areas such as Greater Manchester and south Yorkshire, they had been driven from a host of smaller cities and towns as well. Nowhere was this more evident than along the south coast, where Labour or the LibDems had captured Dover, Hastings, Brighton, Hove, Portsmouth (Southampton was already Labour's), Exeter, Torbay and Plymouth. Elsewhere there were shire towns and cities – Gloucester, Worcester, Chester, Bedford, Oxford, Northampton – all won by Labour. Much of London's hinterland to the north and east was now painted red and, as for the capital itself, it was transformed. The Conservatives began the night with 41 of the 74 Greater London seats; they finished it with 11.

Now one of the few remaining blanks on the map was filled in, as Falmouth and Camborne declared its result. This was the seat of the Olympic double-gold medallist, Sebastian Coe, who took it first in 1992 with a slim majority over the Liberal Democrats. Famous, personable and widely respected as a sportsman, Coe seemed to have the makings of a real asset to the Tories nationally, but for some reason he was never used in that way. Instead he spent the latter part of the parliament as a junior whip and as such was prevented by party rules from making public political statements. The exception was constituency business, but here again Coe failed to make a big impression, and his best hope in defending his seat was that the LibDems and Labour, both mounting strong challenges, would cancel each other out.

Labour's Candy Atherton, a journalist and former mayor of Islington in London, was always confident of jumping from third to first place. Selected from an all-women shortlist in 1995 to fight what was target seat number 50, she had had strong backing from the national party. It was from here on the first day of the campaign that a windswept John Prescott launched his national coach tour of the so-called 'key seats'. Falmouth was a contest where the key to success lay in convincing non-Tory voters that their best bet was Labour – what party strategists called the 'squeeze message'. (This is not subtle: a typical 'squeeze' leaflet would show two racehorses approaching the finishing line, above the words, 'It's a two-horse race'. The third party, by implication, had no hope.) This was a game the LibDems could play as well. Atherton thought things were going very well until a week before polling day, when the local press reported that an opinion poll showed the LibDems ahead in the constituency. The report was challenged, denied and defended, but Atherton was sure it had done her cause a lot of damage.

In the event, she still won, and Sebastian Coe was the eleventh of the original Dicey Dozen to fall under Peter Snow's cliff (Michael Howard was the sole survivor). The Falmouth figures were close, and interesting. Atherton polled 18,000 votes, Coe 15,000 and the LibDem 13,500. The surprise was the showing of the Referendum Party candidate, the millionaire Peter de Savary, who received 3,500 votes, or enough – if they had been cast for Coe – to have made the difference. It was a rare case: of the 547 candidates fielded by Sir James Goldsmith's party, 505 lost their deposits. In all, they received 800,000 votes, or 2.6 per cent.

Labour captured Lancaster and Wyre (target 111), but failed by just 238 votes to take Lichfield (125). A long series of recounts was also under way in Kettering (127) and here, eventually, Labour's Philip Sawford scraped in. It was a famous victory – or at least it would have been if it had not come so late as to be an afterthought – for the defeated Tory was Roger Freeman, another Cabinet Minister.

In his pinstripe suit and with his grey hair always neatly parted and combed, Freeman looks the part of a City gent from around 1970, which is precisely what he was back then. He entered parliament (like so many other people now leaving it) in 1983 and made his biggest public splash when as a junior transport minister he said a privatized rail service could offer 'a cheap and cheerful service for typists and a more luxurious service for civil servants and businessmen'. Despite this revealing slip he acquired a reputation as that most prized of Tory assets, a safe pair of hands, and as such made his way into Cabinet under John Major. He was Chancellor of the Duchy of Lancaster, a mysterious job which seemed mainly to involve him in trying to dig Douglas Hogg out of the holes he threw himself into as he struggled with the BSE crisis. Kettering had looked a safe enough seat for Freeman, and he had had a majority of 12,000 in 1992. But after a very long night including four recounts and a short interlude for recuperation, the Minister finished with 24,461 votes and Sawford with 24,650 – a Labour majority of 189. The Referendum Party candidate won 1,500 votes.

In all the years between the landslide of 1945 and 1997, through 13 general elections, just six serving Cabinet Ministers had lost their seats. They included Anthony Barber in 1964, Shirley Williams in 1979 and Chris Patten in 1992. Now seven had gone in a single night. Of the 21 politicians who sat around the famous Downing Street table for John Major's final Cabinet meeting, one was a peer and one did not seek re-election. Just 12 of the remaining 19 had held on to their seats. Defeated alongside the Ministers, incidentally, were no fewer than 20 knights, one lord (James Douglas-Hamilton, the younger son of a duke), two dames and a lady (Olga Maitland). Besides being rather humbler, the new parliament would also be much younger and much more female. Where previously there had been 57 women MPs, there were now 120, thanks in large measure to Labour's women-only shortlists.

At 6 a.m., after eight hours on air, the Dimblebys and their studio teams on BBC and ITV took a break. Jonathan, having earlier announced his wish to change his shirt, said he was off for 'a bit of kip'. David was more formal, announcing 'the end of a dramatic night in British politics' and inviting us to tune in again later in the morning for the next phase of the transfer of power. Both men, and their teams, had performed wonders. Even when the change it brings is modest, election night is a volatile television experience in which politics and broadcasting interact in a most unusual way. On this night, which David Dimbleby likened to that 'night to remember' when the *Titanic* sank, there had been enough historic change for eight days of television, let alone eight hours. Snow, Paxman, Brunson, Stewart and the rest had already run a marathon; they would be back on the road to resume the race in just four hours' time.

The Blairs, too, drew the line at 6 a.m., leaving the Festival Hall for their home in Islington. They managed just a couple of hours' sleep before Alastair Campbell, somehow briefly separated from them, turned up at 9 a.m. to work on yet another speech. At 11.30 a growing crowd outside saw an official Daimler pull up. Just after noon, while John Major was leaving Buckingham Palace after presenting his resignation to the Queen, Tony Blair and his wife appeared, got into the car and promptly got out again for a quick walkabout among the crowd on Richmond Avenue, N1. It was the first cheering and flag-waving moment in a day that came to resemble a royal wedding or a coronation. Everywhere they went, the Blairs seemed to be borne along by the noise and colour and excitement of throngs of well-wishers. By 12.30 they were at the Palace, where Tony was invited by the monarch to form his government. And then it was on to Downing Street.

John Major, departing a little earlier, had produced the rabbit out of his hat. 'If I may,' he said in his final speech as Prime Minister outside the door of Number 10, 'I would like to clear up one area of speculation that I know has been abroad a little over the last few days. I have been a Member of Parliament for 18 years. I have been a member of the government for 14 years, of the Cabinet for 10 years and Prime Minister since 1990. When the curtain falls it is time to get off the stage – and that is what I propose to do.' He would cease to be leader of the Conservative Party, he explained, as soon as they could pick a replacement, and now he would like a little privacy as he proposed to attend a cricket match at the Oval.

The final 100 yards of Tony Blair's journey into Downing

15. Tony Blair and Cherie work their way into Downing Street.

Street were covered on foot. The Daimler stopped well short of the steel gates – symbolic memorial to Margaret Thatcher – and he and Cherie once again worked their way along the crowd barriers to the sound of 'To-ny! To-ny! To-ny!' Many of those shouting were Labour Party workers who had brought with them their children decked out in T-shirts declaring: 'Britain just got better!' Union flags were everywhere. It seemed an age before the Blairs reached the heart of the little street and broke off for him to make his first speech as Prime Minister, the first speech by a British Labour prime minister since the days of Jim Callaghan, who lost office 18 years earlier, almost to the day.

Speeches of any kind in Downing Street are a novelty. In days of old, when this was a public highway (albeit a rarefied one, and a cul-de-sac), the prime minister might stop at his doorstep on the way in or out to share a thought with the waiting press, but there was rarely anything more formal. That's the way it was when a victorious Harold Wilson said: 'We've got a job of work to do and we're going to get on with it.' And that is the way it was when Thatcher produced her famous lines from St Francis of Assisi about harmony and discord. But the needs of security, dignity and the television industry dictated a different approach, and now, on all sorts of occasions, a podium is erected in the middle of the country's best-known private street for the PM to air his thoughts. The viewing public may have the impression there is an audience on the spot, but behind the cameras there is barely a pavement's width to accommodate the Press. The street is effectively a studio, or even a film set.

Tony Blair, speaking to the nation he now led, began this inaugural address with a tribute to the dignity, courage and 'essential decency' of John Major. Then, one by one, he touched all the same buttons as the Festival Hall speech the night before: we will govern as New Labour; we will keep our promises on health and education; we will work with business to create a dynamic economy; we will clean up politics; we will govern in the interests of all; we will unite the nation. He offered just one oratorical flourish, promising that this would be 'a government of practical measures in pursuit of noble causes'. And he concluded: 'Today, enough of talking – it is time now to *do*.' With that he turned towards the famous black door and (after a final family photocall) the new era began.

Two postscripts remain. In Northern Ireland – another parallel political universe but one that is even more distant than Tatton – the election threw up just a couple of changes, but they were significant ones. The Major years here had been momentous. A dramatic confluence of events in 1994 had led to the first sustained ceasefire, with both the IRA and loyalist paramilitary organizations setting aside their weapons. After the failure to agree terms for the entry of Sinn Fein into peace talks, however, the IRA returned to conflict with a bomb in the London Docklands early in 1996, followed by another in the heart of Manchester. Nevertheless the Major government pressed ahead with its peace process, holding elections to a peace forum. In these Sinn Fein did well, and the question now was how well they would do in Westminster elections and how much ground they would make up on the SDLP in the contest to be the main nationalist party.

When the votes had been counted, all the familiar Unionists – Ian Paisley, David Trimble, Ken Maginnis, Martin Smyth, Peter Robinson – were re-elected, and most of the obscure ones too. John Hume, Seamus Mallon and Eddie McGrady of the SDLP were also returned. But in Belfast West the Sinn Fein president, Gerry Adams, won back the seat he had lost in 1992 to the SDLP's Joe Hendron, while his Sinn Fein colleague Martin McGuinness captured the much-altered Mid Ulster constituency from William McCrea of the Democratic Unionist Party. McGuinness polled 20,000 votes, McCrea 18,000 and the SDLP candidate 11,000. These were important and symbolic advances: Sinn Fein had two MPs and 16 per cent of the Northern Ireland vote. But the SDLP did not have too much to be sorry about, since it retained a big lead over Sinn Fein in the popular vote, with 24 per cent. As for the assorted unionists, their combined tally of votes was little changed, at just a whisker under 50 per cent.

The other unfinished business of the 1997 general election was Winchester where, at the moment of Blair's entry into Number 10, the longest count of the post-war years still had five hours to run. This was a contest between a high-flying junior minister, Gerry Malone, and a Liberal Democrat of 33, Mark Oaten. There had been nothing in advance of the election to suggest that this would be anything other than a routine 'Con hold' result, but it turned out very differently.

Oaten, a lobbying and public relations man, contested his home-town seat of Watford in 1992 and came a poor third. He expected to do a bit better in Winchester, but that was the limit of his ambition. 'I was selected in 1995 and we moved down there to live in the constituency,' he recalls. 'My wife was from the area and wanted to go back, and I had persuaded her that I would have just one more go at an election. I knew I could fight a good campaign but I was pretty sure I'd lose by about 3,000 votes.'

Malone is that rare thing, a Glasgow Irish Catholic who grew up to be a Conservative. A lawyer and journalist, he was MP for an Aberdeen seat in 1983–7, but lost that and switched to safer territory south of the border in 1992, replacing the controversial Winchester Tory, John Browne, who had been de-selected. Seriously ambitious and upwardly mobile, Malone was best known in office as a tough-talking defender of health service reforms – Mr Nasty to Virginia Bottomley's Ms Nice. He had a majority after boundary changes in Winchester of 9,000.

As if things were not bad enough for Oaten, he found himself standing against the country's most notorious spoiler candidate, Richard Huggett. It was Huggett who cost the LibDems victory in a European Parliament contest by standing as a 'Literal Democrat'; now he was in Winchester, offering himself as 'Liberal Democrat Top Choice for Parliament' candidate. After desperate but unsuccessful efforts to have Huggett disqualified, Oaten found that the best he could do was change his own label on the ballot paper to 'Liberal Democrat Paddy Ashdown Leader'.

For all his pessimism, though, Oaten found the campaign went well for him, and as he watched the national opinion polls he perked up. 'The very first time I really thought we could win was on polling day in the afternoon. We had been up since the crack of dawn and done all our leafleting, and I began to think, "This could be tight. It could be down to a couple of hundred votes." At that moment we decided to change our plans and pour all our effort into the last few hours. By 9 p.m. we were doing things you wouldn't normally do, like giving lifts to the polling stations to people who had just had operations. It was a real last push.'

He was home in time for the exit poll. Winchester was a straight fight with the Conservatives and he wanted to see the Tories below 30 per cent. It looked like they were. If Winchester's voters had deserted the Tories like that, he was in. But the count, which he attended virtually from the start, proved painfully slow, and the national outcome was clear even before the local and national ballot papers in Winchester had been separated. 'I had somebody by a television noting down the key results and sending them in to me on little chits. I could see that the political landscape of the country was changing. All my friends were getting in, and their swings would have been enough for me, but we had not even started.'

The signs were promising, though. Watching the ballot papers come out for verification, Oaten's team had the impression that he was well ahead in the city areas. If the rural vote was not too much lower, he had a chance. 'I was really sweating,' he says. Once the counting began it was clear how close it was. 'I watched the piles go up neck and neck: 3,000, 6,000, 7,000, 10,000, 12,000, 17,000 – we were level all the way. Then we started looking around the tables for stray piles. "Are those Oatens? And what are those?" It was a scramble. We got down to the last one, and they did the totals. I was 290 ahead. The returning officer said

16. *Winchester: the longest count of the post-war years.*

there was room for doubt so there would be a recount. It was awful. I was the MP, but I wasn't.'

There was much worse to come. The recount was pretty brisk but no less tense, and it turned the result around. 'I knew the line on the table my votes had to get to and I just didn't get there. Malone ended up 22 votes ahead.' Oaten was devastated. 'I felt like I had been an MP for an hour.' Across the room he saw Richard Huggett, the 'Liberal Democrat Top Choice', who had polled 640 votes – more than enough to make the difference. Oaten walked over and had words.

It was now 7.30 a.m. Tony Blair's 'new dawn' speech was already history but Winchester still did not have its MP. There would have to be another count, but where and when? The tellers were exhausted; the journalists were falling asleep; the council election votes were waiting to be counted and, most pressing of all, the hall was needed shortly for a wedding. An adjournment was agreed. Oaten went home with his wife intending to get some sleep – they had been up well over 24 hours – but it was hopeless. 'The phone never stopped ringing. People just couldn't understand the delay. Somebody rang me to say they thought their Ceefax must be bust and could I tell them the result. It was all so bizarre. I sat there watching Tony Blair go to the Palace and I still didn't know whether I was in or not.'

Counting resumed at 2 p.m. with a fresh team of tellers and under extremely strict new procedures. There was no Press, and virtual silence, and the work proceeded at a snail's pace. There was none of the bank-teller's prestidigitation; every paper was picked up individually, scrutinized and carefully placed on the appropriate pile. Every pile was counted and re-counted relentlessly. Agents haggled over every nuance of the pencil marks on the spoiled papers. Party workers checked their own bundles and

17. Winchester, the evening after the night before, and Mark Oaten victorious.

their opponent's. It was now, as they stood shoulder to shoulder thumbing through bundles, that Oaten and Malone exchanged words for the first time. 'This is ridiculous and undignified, isn't it?' Oaten said. Malone agreed.

It was after 6 p.m. that the counting stopped. At first, nobody was told the outcome but the candidates and their agents. The total for Oaten was 26,100. The total for Malone was 26,098. The margin was just 2 votes. The Conservatives did not ask for a recount. After the longest count, here was another record: the narrowest victory in 87 years, since H. E. Duke won Exeter for the Tories by a single vote in 1910. There had been a swing of 7.36 per cent from Conservative to Liberal Democrat and the merest whisker less would not have been enough. If a single LibDem vote had gone to Malone instead, it would have been a tie. Everyone present was utterly astonished.

The world at large, however, did not yet know, and the BBC *Six O'Clock News* was running. Outside, in Winchester's Guildhall Square, a crowd had been building up all day in the knowledge that something extraordinary was going on, and by now they were several hundred strong and the street had been closed off. The High Sheriff decided to read the result to them from a balcony. All the candidates were asked to troop out behind him and to remain as calm as possible to enable him to complete his announcement in an orderly fashion. 'People out there thought I had lost,' Oaten says. 'I kept a completely straight face, so straight that somebody said later they wouldn't like to play me at poker. But when the numbers were read out the place went berserk. They were cheering, they were roaring, they were crying. I made a speech thanking everybody, and Gerry Malone was gracious. He said one vote would have been enough, and I had won by two.'

*

With the last result in, this was the state of the parties:

Party	Vote	Share (%)	MPs elected	Change from '92
Labour	13,509,543	43.2	418	+147
Conservative	9,602,989	30.7	165	−171
Liberal Democrat	5,242,907	16.8	46	+26
Ulster Unionist	258,349		10	0
Scottish National	621,540		6	+3
Plaid Cymru	161,030		4	0
SDLP	190,814		3	−1
Sinn Fein	126,921		2	+2
Democratic Unionist	107,348		2	−1
UK Unionist	12,817		1	+1
Independent (Bell)	29,354		1	+1
Speaker			1	+1

The general election of 1997 was over.

An election of records and superlatives

Tony Blair, at 43, became the youngest Prime Minister since Lord Liverpool in 1812.

Labour's total of 418 seats was the party's highest ever.

Its total of 13.5 million votes was its highest since 1951.

Its share of the vote, at 43 per cent, was its highest since 1966.

The Liberal Democrats' total of seats, 46, was the highest for any third party since the Liberals won 56 in 1929.

With 165 seats, the Conservatives had their lowest tally since 1906.

Their 9.6 million votes were the party's fewest since 1929.

At 30.7 per cent, their share of the vote was the lowest since 1832.

It was the first time since 1906 that the Conservatives won no seats in Wales.

The Conservatives had never before failed to win a single seat in Scotland.

The number of Cabinet Ministers to lose their seats, seven,

was the highest since 1906 (when eight, including Arthur Balfour, the Tory Prime Minister, were defeated).

The number of women returned, at 120, was the highest ever. Of these, 101 were Labour members.

Sunderland South produced the quickest result on record, in 46 minutes.

The LibDem margin of victory in Winchester, of two votes, was the narrowest in any constituency since 1910.

Martin Bell was the first independent to sit for a British constituency since 1950.

The nine black and Asian MPs elected is the highest number ever.

Turnout in the election, at 71.4 per cent, was the lowest since 1935.

Visit Penguin on the Internet
and browse at your leisure

- ◆ preview sample extracts of our forthcoming books
- ◆ read about your favourite authors
- ◆ investigate over 10,000 titles
- ◆ enter one of our literary quizzes
- ◆ win some fantastic prizes in our competitions
- ◆ e-mail us with your comments and book reviews
- ◆ instantly order any Penguin book

and masses more!

'To be recommended without reservation ... a rich and rewarding on-line experience' – Internet Magazine

www.penguin.co.uk

READ MORE IN PENGUIN

READ MORE IN PENGUIN

POLITICS AND SOCIAL SCIENCES

Accountable to None Simon Jenkins

'An important book, because it brings together, with an insider's authority and anecdotage, both a narrative of domestic Thatcherism and a polemic against its pretensions ... an indispensable guide to the corruptions of power and language which have sustained the illusion that Thatcherism was an attack on "government"' – *Guardian*

The Feminine Mystique Betty Friedan

'A brilliantly researched, passionately argued book – a time bomb flung into the Mom-and-Apple-Pie image ... Out of the debris of that shattered ideal, the Women's Liberation Movement was born' – Ann Leslie

The New Untouchables Nigel Harris

Misrepresented in politics and in the media, immigration is seen as a serious problem by the vast majority of people. In this ground-breaking book, Nigel Harris draws on a mass of evidence to challenge existing assumptions and examines migration as a response to changes in the world economy.

Political Ideas Edited by David Thomson

From Machiavelli to Marx – a stimulating and informative introduction to the last 500 years of European political thinkers and political thought.

Structural Anthropology Volumes 1–2 Claude Lévi-Strauss

'That the complex ensemble of Lévi-Strauss's achievement ... is one of the most original and intellectually exciting of the present age seems undeniable. No one seriously interested in language or literature, in sociology or psychology, can afford to ignore it' – George Steiner

Invitation to Sociology Peter L. Berger

Without belittling its scientific procedures Professor Berger stresses the humanistic affinity of sociology with history and philosophy. It is a discipline which encourages a fuller awareness of the human world ... with the purpose of bettering it.